Clinical (er
and Higher Education

Clinical counselling in ... ... is different from many other forms of therapy in that the counsellor's work is, in most cases, to assist the primary educational task, rather than be an end in itself. Yet little has been written about the implications or possibilities of the complex relationship between clinical work and context.

In *Clinical Counselling in Further and Higher Education*, a range of well-known contributors show how they work with the dynamics of the context to bring about therapeutic change. It will prove invaluable to students, practising counsellors and psychotherapists.

The first two chapters consider the parallel contribution made by the process of learning and the therapeutic endeavour to the student's emotional development, and the significance of the organisation for the role of the counsellor. The next five chapters are primarily concerned with clinical issues such as the dynamic aspects of the Educational Cycle; how different models of counselling can benefit students, staff and organisation; the potential of brief counselling, whether psychodynamic in orientation or cognitive behavioural; and the possibilites afforded by therapeutic groups. The last three chapters return to the wider context to describe demographic changes in the student population, the impact of the broader social context and, finally, the different research models in use today and how they relate to 'real life in a university or college counselling service'.

John Lees runs the postgraduate counselling training course at the University of Greenwich. He is UKRC registered independent counsellor, a member of the British Association for Psychoanalytic and Psychodynamic Supervision, and Editor of the journal *Psychodynamic Counselling*; **Alison Vaspe** is a BAC accredited counsellor at King's College, London, and manages the counselling service at the Marylebone Health Centre. She is Commissioning Editor of *Psychodynamic Counselling*.

Contributors: Elsa Bell; Alex Coren; Ann E. Heyno; Nigel Humphrys; Colin Lago; Peter Mark; Robert May; Lesley Parker; Gabrielle Rifkind; Peter Ross; Eileen Smith; Suzanna Stein.

Clinical Counselling in Context
Series editor: John Lees

This series of key texts examines the unique nature of counselling in a wide range of clinical settings. Each book shows how the context in which counselling takes place has profound effects on the nature and outcome of the counselling practice, and encourages clinical debate and dialogue.

Clinical Counselling in Context
An Introduction
Edited by John Lees

Clinical Counselling in Primary Care
Edited by John Lees

Clinical Counselling in Further and Higher Education
Edited by John Lees and Alison Vaspe

Clinical Counselling in Further and Higher Education

Edited by
John Lees and Alison Vaspe

London and New York

First published 1999 by Routledge
11 New Fetter Lane, London EC4P 4EE

Simultaneously published in the USA and Canada
by Routledge
29 West 35th Street, New York, NY 10001

© 1999 Edited by John Lees and Alison Vaspe

Typeset in Goudy by
Keystroke, Jacaranda Lodge, Wolverhampton
Printed and bound in Great Britain by
Clays Ltd, St. Ives PLC

British Library Cataloguing in Publication Data
A catalogue record for this book is available from the British Library

Library of Congress Cataloging in Publication Data
A catalogue record for this book has been requested

ISBN 0–415–19280–3 (hbk)
ISBN 0–415–19281–1 (pbk)

Contents

Notes on contributors

Elsa Bell has worked as a counsellor with young people since 1975 and in student counselling since 1979. She has been Head of Counselling at Oxford University since 1990. She is former Chair of the Association of Student Counselling and the British Association for Counselling, and is currently Chair of the United Kingdom Register Executive Committee and the Counselling and Psychotherapy Development Group of the Lead Body for Advice, Guidance, Counselling and Psychotherapy. She is a fellow of Kellogg College, Oxford, the British Association for Counselling and the Royal Society of Arts.

Alex Coren trained with the British Association of Psychotherapists and has worked in secondary and higher education both in the state and independent sectors. He is the author of *A Psychodynamic Approach to Education* and is currently Deputy Head of the University of Oxford Counselling Service.

Ann E. Heyno is head of the Counselling and Advisory Service at the University of Westminster, where she has been a student counsellor for the past nineteen years. For eight years she was course organizer of the Diploma in Student Counselling at Birkbeck, where she is now senior tutor on the M.Sc. in Psychodynamic Counselling (Student Specialism). Her background is in journalism and teaching and she has worked in a school and in child guidance. She was an executive member of the Association for Student Counselling for five years.

She is co-author of *Helping the Unemployed Professional* and has contributed papers at various national and European conferences. Publications include: *Student Success and the Institution*; *Adhesive Learning*; *Pelvic Affiliation in a Perspex Society*; *Psychodynamic Counselling in Practice in Psychological Counselling in Higher Education, A European Overview*; and 'Student counselling: the wailing wall or a force for change?' in *Advocacy, Counselling and Mediation in Case Work*. A graduate of Trinity College, Dublin, she has a diploma in Psycho-dynamic Counselling from Birkbeck.

Nigel Humphrys is a BAC accredited counsellor presently working as Senior Student Counsellor at the University of Leeds. Nigel trained as a counsellor in the United States and while there became interested in cross-cultural issues in counselling. On returning to the UK he worked as Overseas Student Adviser at the University of Hertfordshire and while there founded the Association of International Student Advisers. Prior to his present position Nigel was the Manager of the Student Counselling and Advice Centre at London Guildhall University. He is presently working on a research project involving the University of British Columbia, Canada, Griffiths University, Australia, South Bank University, UK and the University of Leeds, looking into the acquisition of cultural competencies of international students.

Colin Lago is the Director of the Counselling Service at the University of Sheffield. He is a Fellow of the British Association for Counselling and former Chair of the Association of Student Counselling. He has previously written books and articles on student counselling, trans-cultural counselling and international students and his co-authored new book is on the management of counselling and psychotherapy services.

John Lees is a counsellor and supervisor. He is also Senior Lecturer in Counselling and Pathway Leader for the M.Sc. in Therapeutic Counselling course at the University of Greenwich. His clinical work includes general practice counselling and private practice. He has also worked in student counselling. He is editor of *Psychodynamic Counselling* and numerous articles in the field of counselling.

Peter Mark is a group analyst/student counsellor at King's College, London and is also employed as a senior group analyst at the Parkside Clinic, London (NHS). He is an experiential group conductor at the Institute of Group Analysis and the London Centre of Psychotherapy and supervisor of group therapy at the Westminster Pastoral Foundation, and has many years experience as an organisational consultant teacher and staff group facilitator.

Prior to his psychotherapy training, Peter worked for twenty years in the Probation Service, where he was Director of a therapeutic community for offenders and specialized in group work with sex offenders.

Robert May, Ph.D., is a clinical psychologist and Director of the Counselling and Mental Health Service at Amherst College, in Amherst, Massachusetts. He has worked as a psychotherapist at several colleges and universities and has written numerous papers on psychotherapy in general and on work with college and university students in particular. He spent a year as a Visiting Attached Staff Member in the Adult Department of the Tavistock Clinic and has presented papers at conferences on college and university counselling at the Tavistock Clinic and at City University in London.

Lesley Parker is currently employed by Cambridge University Counselling Service. She has been a student counsellor since 1980, having previously worked at the Universities of Edinburgh and Hertfordshire. Since 1995 she has been chair of the AUCC research committee, and involved in various research projects.

Gabrielle Rifkind is trained as a group analyst probation officer and art therapist. She has run groups in different settings for the past twenty years. This has included working in the NHS and Probation Service and working within organizations. Three years ago she moved to working in the university and was interested in how to adapt group analytic ideas to this setting.

She is also a practising artist and journalist and is particularly interested in how creativity brings about change.

Peter Ross is a chartered counselling psychologist and chartered occupational psychologist. He is Head of the Counselling Service at the University of Reading. He has been a member of the Executive Committee of the Association for University and College Counselling and Chair of the Heads of University Counselling Services. He has published widely in the field of belief systems.

Eileen Smith is Head of the Counselling Service at the University of Hertfordshire and a UKRC registered independent counsellor. She is the editor of *Integrity and Change* and co-author of *Long-term Counselling*.

Suzanna Stein is Head of Counselling, Advisory and Health in the student services department of the University of Greenwich, London. She also lectures part-time on the M.Sc. in Therapeutic Counselling in the School of Social Sciences, which she helped to develop. She has been working in education for twenty-eight years. Also at the University of Greenwich, she has developed the Counselling Skills for Teachers and Managers course in the School of Education, the trainee counselling programme within student services and the complementary therapy provision which is allied to the counselling service.

Alison Vaspe studied music and worked in publishing before training as a counsellor at Westminster Pastoral Foundation and Birkbeck College, London. She has an MA in Psychoanalytic Psychotherapy from the

Guild of Psychotherapists/University of Hertfordshire, for which her research subject was counselling women medical students. She works as a counsellor at King's College, London, and at the Marylebone Health Centre. She is also Commissioning Editor of the journal *Psychodynamic Counselling*.

Introduction

This volume is part of a series of books which examines the way in which counselling is applied in different occupational settings. The series as a whole is based on the notion that there is a complex interrelationship between clinical work and the context in which it takes place. It is felt that, while the context may provide many dilemmas for counsellors, it also contains features which may help the therapeutic process – indeed that the sophistication of clinical counselling lies, to some extent, in its ability to work with the complexities of the context as a whole and, in particular, the nature of the setting in which it takes place. So what are the features of clinical counselling in further and higher education that distinguish it from other settings? In what way is it different and unique?

An obvious feature of clinical counselling in further and higher education is that therapeutic work is a secondary task of the organization. The main task of educational institutions is learning (although the cynic might say that it is to make money, and many academics might put research above teaching in their list of priorities). So one can reasonably make the assumption that the therapeutic work provided by counselling centres or student service departments is meant, at least as far as most organizations are concerned, to assist and further the primary educational task rather than be an end in itself. This distinguishes it from many other settings that are covered by this series. In primary care, for example, the primary task is increasingly to attend to the health of the whole person, physical and emotional, and so corresponds with the aims of clinical counselling. Thus an important question for this book has been: does it matter that the aims of counsellors and the organizations in which they work do not entirely correspond? And if so, what are the implications for clinical counselling in this setting?

One possible outcome of these differing aims is that counsellors may come into conflict with the organization. The educational authorities are primarily concerned with providing a creative learning environment, making money or doing research (or, in reality, a combination of these) while the clinical counsellor is primarily concerned with therapeutic work. Government, managers, administrators, lecturers and academics may well end up pulling in a different direction to counsellors. Yet it is also possible that this can have a more creative side to it. For example, Freud encountered many obstacles as he was trying to develop psychoanalysis, but managed to turn them to his advantage. When he found that his patients were reacting to him in an exaggerated manner he saw it first as an obstacle. But, as he developed his ideas, he began to see it as an advantage. He gradually formed the view that these exaggerated responses (or what later became known as transferences) provided the opportunity for many of the patient's neurotic tendencies to be analysed, understood and interpreted in the consulting room. It was better to be able to do this in the here and now rather than at second hand (Freud 1914).

These two strands – namely the potential conflict between consulting room and context and the possibility that the different aims of the two can be used to our therapeutic advantage – run through all of the chapters in this volume to some extent. This is clearly apparent in the first two chapters which, in a sense, set the scene for the whole book. In the first chapter, entitled 'The role of education in the role of counselling in further and higher education', Elsa Bell brings a wide-angled lens to bear on the parallel contribution made by the process of learning and, where necessary, the therapeutic endeavour to the student's emotional development. Citing Irene Caspari, who believed that 'psychoanalysis is not the only way to make therapeutic use of the child's playing', she extends the notion of 'play' to include a process that can take place not just between counsellor and client, but also between teacher and student.

Robert May in 'Doing clinical work in a college or university: how does the context matter?' meanwhile, looks at the significance of the structure and type of organization to the role of the counsellor. He asks how the counsellor can negotiate the inevitable tensions between them. What does the institution want, and how much of that is it appropriate for counsellors to give? What, on the other hand, does the counsellor want, and how much of that is communicable to and supportable by the employing organization which has to prioritize its budget allocations? Looking to such outer world realities, he acknowledges the inner aspects of this tension and emphasizes the counsellor's need constantly to find a way of managing the projections, counter-projections and projective identifications of the organization. Thus, as well as exploring the two fundamental strands of the book – the tensions and potential advantages of working in an organization – these first two chapters also highlight the part played in the inner world of the psyche by the outer world of pragmatism and concrete reality.

The next five chapters are primarily concerned with clinical issues. Ann Heyno, in 'Cycles in the mind: clinical technique and the educational cycle', reminds us of the need to hold in mind 'interaction between the client's emotional experiences as students and their internal reality as individuals'. She examines certain dynamic aspects of the educational setting, with its round of terms and holidays, exams, beginnings and endings, and notes their impact on the student's inner world. In so doing she shows how, by working with the rhythms and realities of the setting, rather than against or in ignorance of them, the counsellor can find a fuller understanding of the student's difficulties. Suzanna Stein, in 'Student empowerment, staff support and organizational stress', also adopts a creative approach to the setting, showing how different models of counselling can benefit students, staff and organization. She examines the range of different interventions – counselling, consultation to staff, exam preparation and staff counselling – that can be brought into play in response to the different needs of the organization. Her approach, based on Egan's integrative model, is pragmatic and problem-solving.

Similar contrasts in clinical approach mark the next two articles. Alex Coren, in 'Brief psychodynamic counselling in educational settings', describes an approach to short-term work in an educational setting. He returns to the question addressed by Elsa Bell – how to harness the creative possibilities of working as a counsellor in a context of academic study – and shows how an imaginative understanding of the student's age and developmental issues, together with their expectations of adults and their choice of academic subject, can make brief counselling the treatment of choice for many. Peter Ross, in 'Focusing the work: a cognitive-behavioural approach', also looks at time-limited work, here from the point of view of a counsellor working with cognitive behavioural techniques. He points to the importance of research findings in organizations' understanding of what can be done for different problems. Whereas Alex Coren adopts an interpretive approach and describes how therapeutic interventions can take into account the dynamics of the whole setting, Peter Ross unpacks the 'self-talk' of students in a discourse designed to help them defuse their immediate anxieties. Both, however, show the importance for clinical effectiveness of respecting the culture of the setting and individual modes of thought and understanding.

In the last of the specifically clinical chapters, Mark and Rifkind in 'Establishing group psychotherapy in a student counselling service', describe the benefits to student counselling services of providing therapeutic groups for students. Describing their own experience of introducing groups into an unfamiliar setting, they show how a thoughtful approach and careful selection can allow students opting to join slow–open groups the experience of recognizing their own and others' feelings and ways of relating, to mutual therapeutic effect.

The final three chapters return to the wider context. Lago and Humphrys, in 'Issues of difference in further and higher education', describe the demographic changes that have taken place in colleges and universities in recent years. They look at the changing face of the student body – in particular difference and diversity both within individuals, and as apparent from skin, age, nationality, cultural grouping or ethnicity, age, gender and sexual orientation. How are counsellors to meet and recognize the diverse needs of this heterogeneous group of individuals? Eileen Smith, on the other hand, in 'No client (and no counsellor) is an island: attending to the culture of the educational setting', looks to the need to be aware of the prevailing emotional climate, not just within the individual organization but also in the wider social context. Tracing the different nuances and meanings of the word 'culture', she describes the impact of outer changes on inner worlds, and shows how individuals – not just students, but staff and counsellors also – react or respond to the broader social context.

Finally, Lesley Parker in 'Evaluation of clinical counselling in educational settings: preparing for the future' considers the progress made by student counsellors in auditing and evaluating their services. She considers the different research models in use today and explores how they relate to 'real life in a university or college counselling service'. While acknowledging the difficulty of matching research to the subtleties, complexities and sometimes uncertainties of practice, she none the less regrets the resistance of counsellors to carrying out research that might genuinely help them think about, justify and communicate how they are carrying out the task their organizations pay them for.

John Lees and Alison Vaspe
June 1998

Acknowledgements

We should like to thank the following for advice and suggestions: Nick Barwick, Elsa Bell, Trudy Chapman, Zack Eleftheriadou, Adrian Lenthall, Professor John McLeod, Dr Stirling Moorey, Suzanna Stein, Michael Tait, and especially Paul Terry.

1   The role of education in the role of counselling in further and higher education

Elsa Bell

All counsellors who work in an institutional context must take on board the demands of the organization. The structure, the ethos, the subtle and, at times, not so subtle ways in which influence is exerted, all have an impact on the nature of the counselling relationship. Every time a counsellor meets a client an aspect of the organization is in the room. If it is not recognized, then something vital is missed.

Counsellors in education know that they are working with people at a point of change, and that the deeply held, if sometimes forgotten, desires that this wish for change represents are significant in their work. The context is the meaning, and the very process of education has many therapeutic possibilities that can be enlisted in the work of student counselling services.

An early contribution from psychoanalysis to our understanding of the learning process

While student counsellors come from a number of theoretical backgrounds there is a commonly held view of the importance of the symbolic nature of learning and what this might represent for the development of the student. Much of this understanding comes from the work of Melanie Klein, and although, for example, those trained in the person-centred tradition might not accept the techniques and details of psychoanalytic thinking and practice, Klein's analysis of young children has given a basis from which the process of learning, and particularly the routes by which learning can become inhibited, is understood. The following quotation from 'The role of the school in the libidinal development of the child' is, at one and the same time, both enlightening and, in the words of the author, potentially 'dispiriting'.

> But even the possibility of a good teacher easing the conflict is a very slight one, for limits are set by the child's complex formations,

particularly by his relationship to his father, which determines beforehand his attitudes to school and teacher.

This, however, explains why, where more powerful inhibitions are concerned, the results of even years of pedagogical labour present no relation to the effort expended, while in analysis we often find these inhibitions removed in a comparatively short time and replaced by complete pleasure in learning.

It would be best, therefore, to reverse the process; first of all, an early analysis should remove the inhibitions more or less present in every child, and work at school should start on this foundation. When it has no longer to fritter away its forces in dispiriting attacks upon the children's complexes, the school will be able to achieve fruitful work significant for the development of the child.

(Klein 1975a: 76)

It is enlightening because it shows, in an encapsulated form, the theoretical framework on which many modern student counsellors, particularly those trained within the psychoanalytic tradition, base their work. In it we see Klein demonstrate her contention that a child's capacity for learning is dependent on the quality of sublimatory activity in relation to the amount of inhibition through repression of early, infantile feelings. These infantile feelings are based in the first experiences of being fed and in the natural functions of expelling food.

According to this reading, since a child is unable to distinguish its own 'self' from the surrounding world, it supposes that everything that it feels is of its own making. If something around it makes it feel good then it is because it has made it so, but equally if something makes it feel bad, that too is of its own creation. The world, therefore, is peopled with good and bad objects that are expected to behave in the way the baby has designated them. Since the first object is the mother's breast, and this can alternately be a source of great comfort i.e. food and 'goodness' or great discomfort i.e. no food and 'badness', the child finds itself loving and hating the same object in rapid succession.

The process of interpretation of the two most important physical functions, that of taking in and giving out, plays an important part in the development of mental processes. The phantasies, or ideas, about the need to take in (introject) only good objects in order to feel good, coupled with the natural feeling of pain and 'badness' that the digestive process produces, leads to the notion that somehow the child has taken in its own bad feelings. To feel good again these must be got rid of (projected).

When the child eventually discovers that the good and bad objects of its earlier experiences are, in fact, one and the same person, the mother, it is forced to contemplate ways of holding on to that which it both hates and loves. However, this notion of holding the good and bad in one object is so painful that the baby frequently seeks relief in returning to the position where good and bad are split into separate compartments. The necessity to restore and keep the loved object, so that the internal world feels secure, becomes the major task through childhood and adult life and the capacity to do so determines all aspects of emotional and intellectual development.

In order that this task might be accomplished, the developing child endows the other aspects of its external world with the attributes it perceived in its first 'object' and thus, in a symbolic way, repeats the process of coming to terms with the feelings of love and hate. Klein's version of this complicated mental process, whereby internal conflicts of a primitive nature are dealt with symbolically through activities in the real world, a development of Freud's ideas on sublimation, have, she says, a particular relevance to education. When libido is successfully sublimated, the task of learning is carried out with pleasure but with no awareness of the unconscious associations. When it is unsuccessfully sublimated the associations stir up unacceptable conflicts, and in a defence against these overwhelming conflicts, the learning is inhibited – the symbol is dangerous and must not be used.

But what of the statement that this must be dealt with through analysis if the child is to be able to learn – that the task of the teacher (and we could read 'counsellor') is impossible without this early analysis? Should counsellors feel dispirited by this statement? Later writers have given a basis from which student counsellors have developed their ideas about what, more optimistically, can be dealt with directly through counselling and, indirectly, through the teaching and learning process.

Learning as a both a symbol and a process

Developing from his work on transitional phenomena D.W. Winnicott developed the concept of 'playing' to describe the process whereby a child begins to differentiate between what is subjective, and inside, and what is objective, and outside. His choice of the gerund, or verbal noun, rather than the noun 'play' emphasizes the sense of action and agency inherent in his concept of playing. In 'Playing: a theoretical statement' (1971a) he suggests that playing is natural, healthy and universal and that it has an importance in communication that is entirely its own. He draws the important distinction between play as seen by Klein (1975b) where there is a regression to the instinctual impulses, and his own observations of playing which, he suggests, needs to be studied as a subject on its own and be considered as a concept supplementary to that of sublimation. He poses the idea that the space between the parent and the child, in which playing takes place, becomes the prototype of the space in which future, more adult, creative activity is carried out.

When he defines psychotherapy as taking place 'in the overlap of two areas of playing, that of the patient and the therapist' (1971a: 44), and when he says in *Therapeutic Consultations in Child Psychiatry* (1971b), 'It should be noted that in this work I do not usually make interpretations, but I wait until the essential features of the child's communication has been revealed. Then I talk about the essential feature, but the importance is not my talking so much as the fact that the child has reached something', we begin to see the significance of playing for the teacher and the counsellor. For if therapy can be in the playing itself, and not just in the interpretations given, then there is also a dimension in the playing world of the teacher and student, the counsellor and client, that is potentially therapeutic.

At the same time as Winnicott was developing his concept of playing, Irene Caspari was developing a way of working with children who had learning problems which she called Educational Therapy. Her approach was founded on the idea, also expressed by Winnicott (1971a: 58) that, 'it would be a narrow view to suppose that psychoanalysis is the only way to make therapeutic use of the child's playing'. In 'Techniques of Educational Therapy' (1975) she describes her approach as a therapeutic intervention that combines aspects of carefully programmed teaching, derived from educational theory, linked to psychoanalytic models.

She goes on to describe her method as one that incorporates aspects akin to those in behaviour therapy, such as carefully programmed work, continuous repetition and practice with rewards when the desired goal is reached, although she sees the main difference between her work and that of the behaviourists in the understanding of the use of the educational programme. She sees the educational programme as adaptable and related to the belief that the teacher/child relationship holds many similarities with the mother/child relationship in the feeding situation. Since it is generally understood that successful feeding depends not just on the quality of the relationship between mother and child, but also on the appropriateness of the food, so in the teaching situation the child's ability to take in and digest will be governed, in the main, by three things: the interaction of the teacher and pupil; the degree to which the material is gauged to the pupil's appetite; and whether or not it is presented so that the pupil can take it in.

Although the greater part of Caspari's work was carried out with children who had reading difficulties, a description of her methods gives a graphic indication for the modern counsellor in further and higher education of the possibilities of using educational material, and the learning process, as a therapeutic tool. She points to the symbolic nature of learning through her work in helping children to deal with the symbols that must be mastered in order to reach the level of objectivity at which a book can be read. These ideas are illustrated in her account of work with a boy called Peter.

Peter was aged 13 and of average intelligence, but his reading age was 5 years 6 months. He had learned the sounds of letters and was able to blend three-letter words at times, but could not read unknown words of the same kind in a book. He often knew the sounds and could repeat them in the correct order, but was unable to put them together again. In order to respond to this difficulty the educational therapist used a method known as the 'cutting-up procedure'. The child is given the illustration of a three-letter word with the word beneath it and then invited to cut up the card, cutting through the picture and between the letters, so as to make a jigsaw puzzle.

Caspari reports that on 4 April Peter was given the word CAT on a postcard with the suggestion that he should draw the picture and then cut it up.

> He recognised the word and then drew the picture. Then he started to cut it – commenting on the pain of the animal and saying, 'poor pussy cat – it's lost his head'. He referred to his pussy cat at home and I said maybe he felt bad hurting the cat. He said, no, he had enjoyed it! I then pointed out the word was destroyed and asked him if he could put it together. He did this, and said the sounds and then said the word. He wanted to do another and I suggested the word DOG. He pointed out that this would be GOD spelt backwards.

In subsequent sessions Peter looked at his cut-up picture of the cat and remarked 'poor pussy cat'. He went on to cut up RAT and as he put it together commented that it was better now. He dropped a piece of a cut-up PIG saying it was squealing and alive. He cut up MAN and described it as torn to bits. When the comment was made that the word was also torn to pieces he said that he could put it together again. After he was able to sound out the word GOD he asked how he could draw God. He went on to do it drawing the crucifixion and saying 'that's the end of him'. When he had put it together he put the pieces in his pocket saying 'I'll put God in my pocket. I mustn't lose him.'

She goes on to record that in the session on 9 May Peter wanted to have the envelope with his cut-up pictures. She suggested cutting up some words without pictures but this met with a lack of enthusiasm. She then said he could try another picture if he wanted to and he took a blank card, placing it next to him, and said he would do it later on. He accepted five words for cutting up (rap, set, hid, fog, tub). He did not recognize the words and cut them up, commenting that he would cut straight between the letters instead of making a jigsaw puzzle. He sounded out and synthesized each word. As they packed away Peter picked up the blank card. He wrote COW and drew a rather crude picture. He attacked the card cutting it up with enthusiasm and saying, 'I don't like cows. I don't like beef.' Having cut it up he put it in his envelope and was ready to leave.

Caspari's commentary continues:

> If the process of blending is seen as cutting-up the word and putting it together again, Peter's reaction to the cutting-up procedure indicates that his inability to blend was linked to his great desire to destroy and an equally great fear that it was not possible to put together what was previously destroyed. At the time he was given the cards to cut up he had already experienced that unacceptable feelings could be 'safely' expressed via acting, drawing and modelling. Now he experienced it in connection with the reading process. The sequence suggests that he had to repeat this experience in various ways, for instance, by testing out that bits of the pig were not alive and that the cut-up man could be put together again. The sequence ended with his triumphant destruction of the cow, who obviously represented someone he wanted to destroy and whom he could destroy safely now by symbolisation. After this experience he was able to blend fluently. He had experienced the difference between reality and a symbol, the difference between feelings and actions. He needed to experience that feelings could be expressed in symbols and could now be more at ease with his destructive phantasies. In Peter's case the episode about cutting-up and preserving the word 'god' was also important, although he did not give much information of what this meant to him. Whatever it was it was now cut up and 'safe in his pocket', and in the following session he could synthesise five words without difficulty.
>
> (Caspari 1975: 3–4)

This extract of work with a child is reported in detail because it illustrates many of the factors that student counsellors take into account when thinking about the meaning of education and learning for those whom they see. It uses Klein's ideas that the subject studied can represent primitive internal struggles and that there needs to be a place where the symbolism can be examined if the capacity to study is breaking down. But in addition, it suggests that sometimes something significant happens that does not need to be interpreted. Yet it is still profoundly therapeutic. Peter had 'God' safe in his pocket and this was significant for his progress in his study.

When Winnicott talked of, simply, receiving the communication and talking about what was directly communicated, rather than making an interpretation of the symbolism, he makes it sound all too simple – as if all we have to do is hear. Behind his statement is the body of theoretical knowledge about the quality of the relationship and the capacity of the therapist to contain and hold the therapeutic/transitional space so that the child understands, in a profound way, that the message has been received. Student counsellors attempt to create an environment where symbolic material can be interpreted, if appropriate (Winnicott was not saying that he never made interpretations), but also one where other communications can be heard and valued for their therapeutic importance. Within this framework it is possible to understand that the whole process of learning has possibilities for therapeutic change: that students may be working outside the consulting room to put something 'safely in their pockets'.

Many student counsellors who work in a psychodynamic way have been trained within the tradition of analytic psychotherapy. For some, their training can leave them with the idea that student counselling is something less than 'real psychotherapy' – that their decisions not to work, at times, in a classical way are merely pragmatic and governed by the context. When this is the case they can feel discouraged by the external demands of working in an educational institution and imagine that if the therapeutic work were not interrupted by terms, the need for tutorials and classes to be attended and the ever-present reality of tests and examinations, then a full piece of therapeutic work could be achieved. While anxiety about the legitimacy of their work may be true for some, there are many others who have recognized that student counselling gives an opportunity for a different understanding of what might be included in the therapeutic process. They know that it is not the classical analysis advocated by Klein, but they also know that what they offer is not necessarily less. It is something different that is aided, rather than restricted, by the educational context. This, more inclusive, theory of what might constitute a therapeutic space allows student counsellors to listen for clues as to how students use their work, and their relationships with others in the institution, to support their psychological development. For example, the whole area of how students choose a subject for study is ripe with therapeutic opportunities.

Counselling in the context of the student's experience of learning

If, within the Winnicottian framework, study can be seen as taking place in the transitional space, then we can see that a choice of subject can represent much of the internal world of the student and is a vehicle for this, subjective, experience to be tested against the reality of the external world. It calls for the student to relinquish omnipotent ideas that what s/he creates is magically perfect and to recognize that the subject (or subjective experience) requires control through the manipulation of ideas. It is not completely within their control, but nor is it outside their control. It has a reality of its own and yet is imbued with qualities that are 'me-yet-not-me' and 'you-yet-not-you'.

A question asked about their subject, when students first come for counselling, can reveal information that is useful as a diagnostic tool. How they describe it, and its meaning for them, can indicate how much students are doing for themselves. The historian may be attempting to find links between seemingly unconnected events; the geologist may be building up a picture of the strata of her life; the student of public relations may be deciding what information needs to be private and what can be in the family or public domain. The counsellor can then make decisions about what can judiciously be left to the student's natural capacity to deal with the symbolic and therapeutic possibilities within the chosen subject. Often the message is just heard and understood. Sometimes the message is replayed to students as a means of indicating to them that they are already addressing something that is of fundamental importance to them.

A student at a college of art came for counselling because she was still troubled by the psychological impact on her of facial injuries she had received as a child. In a college where image was central to the work, she felt constantly reminded of her ugliness. She was studying photography and had chosen, as a specialist subject, industrial landscapes. She was determined to show the beauty in places that others would consider to be disfigured.

In some cases the reason for the choice of subject has become so tied up with unconscious processes, and has become such a dangerous symbol, that it is no longer manageable, and a more detailed exploration is required.

A medical student failed some of his first year examinations. This came as a shock to him, and his tutors, because he had a long history of academic success. In counselling he began to understand his reasons for believing that he wanted to study medicine, and some of the reasons why he might have begun, unconsciously, to sabotage his stated desires.

His younger sister was physically handicapped and he had spent most of his life being a good and helpful brother. His contact, through her, with hospitals had suggested to him that this would be a career where he could continue to be helpful to others. At the age of 9 he decided he would be a doctor. He studied hard so that he would be admitted to a good school and then studied even harder so that he would gain the requisite high grades that would take him to medical school.

In counselling he began to discover that as well as benevolent feelings toward his sister he was also angry at the attention she had received and the space she had taken up in the family's life. At a more profound level he was to discover that his attempts to be a good boy had made him eschew the messy and dirty activities that would normally constitute the life of a growing boy. Far from medicine confirming him as a good, clean boy he was now forced to be in touch with the murky and 'dirty' aspects of people's bodies and of his own desires. Until he could reconcile the two he would go on failing in his studies.

Even when students do not come to counselling with a study difficulty, reference to the subject choice can deepen therapeutic understanding.

A physicist came for counselling saying that she was depressed because she did not believe in God. In one session she talked of how the laws of gravity could be understood within the context of the stars we know about. She added that there may well be other stars that have influence of which we are, as yet, unaware. At one level she was expressing her understanding of the therapeutic process. She said it was like developing an equation, a working model, based on evidence that had gradually been uncovered but that in the future the equation might have to be modified in the light of new discoveries. She was also coming to terms with her anger that her father had an illness for which science, as yet, has found no cure – that science, in which she had put so much faith, had let her down.

Perhaps a more controversial aspect of a theory that accepts the therapeutic opportunities in the whole of the educational process, is that of relationships with academic staff and others who contribute to students' progress. Warburton (1995) presents a thoughtful analysis of the difficulties for those who work within organizations in preserving the therapeutic 'frame'. She accepts that counsellors in education will, necessarily, have contact with others in the institution, but sees these contacts as being detrimental to the therapeutic process within the consulting room. Drawing on the work of earlier psychoanalysts and the more recent communicative therapist, Robert Langs, she suggests that even the inevitable, brief contacts with tutors that work in an academic institution requires will have a profound effect on the relationship between the student and the counsellor and thus on the therapeutic work. She concludes that contact with those outside the consulting room, and thus the therapeutic frame, should be kept to the absolute minimum.

A more radical view is that the therapeutic frame is not simply within the counselling room but can be defined as the process of being a student. It would be fanciful, not to say inappropriate, to suppose that educational establishments are set up to offer a therapeutic experience. Nevertheless, if we accept that subject choice, attitudes to the academic year and its demands, and relationships with tutors and colleagues can all have a symbolic as well as real meaning, then counsellors are challenged to develop ways of working with these therapeutic possibilities, in parallel with the relationship within the counselling room.

This is not to suggest that the ethical principles on which the counselling relationship is based should be compromised. The boundaries of confidentiality still have to be preserved and Warburton challenges those who work in this more radical way to pay attention to the ethical principles involved. However the very process of working with students in deciding what information needs to be conveyed to those outside the counselling room, who should convey that information and what this might represent within the counselling relationship, can be used to further the therapeutic process. For example, students who come from troubled backgrounds where communications between parents are so attenuated, or conflictual, that they develop an internal model for relationships that requires them to keep 'parents' apart, can be profoundly helped by the experience of seeing a counsellor and tutor working together. A more benign parental model is introjected and becomes part of a new constellation of internal figures that influence the students' response to relationships and work.

Even more fanciful than supposing the primary task of an educational institution is to be therapeutic, would be to imagine that all tutors should consciously decide to be educational therapists. However, Caspari's model highlights the possibilities for therapeutic change within the teaching relationship itself. This gives a framework within which counsellors can formulate policies in relation to supporting the teaching and pastoral functions of their academic colleagues.

Staff within educational institutions inhabit a complex world that produces many demands. They come into education because they, like their students, have developed a love of their subject, and a desire to teach it, for deeply private reasons. At the same time they are asked to demonstrate their personal engagement with their subject, to perform their academic tasks, in a variety of public ways. The need for external assessment and quality control adds a dimension that, for some, feels like an attack on personal commitment. When published research is seen less as evidence of scholarship and the academic, and personal, development of an individual, and more as a means of gaining corporate status and funding for a department within the national grading system, individual academics can find their motivation, uncomfortably, diluted. If the primary academic task is further diluted with necessary, but increasing, administrative duties the reason for entering academic life can become more distant. Within this context, it would be unfortunate if counsellors were to seem to suggest that academics should move even further away from their primary purpose and add the role of counsellor to their many tasks.

It is no coincidence that, even when counselling services are asked by academic staff to provide courses in counselling, attendance at such courses is often low. This is often explained by the fact that there is, in reality, not enough space in a busy lecturer's timetable for yet another course. It may also be that, despite a sense that they ought to attend, at some level they know they should not. Their task is to teach, research and hold an overview of students' progress. It is not to become a counsellor.

Yet the perpetual requests for counselling courses should not be ignored. They might be more profitably understood as communications that even the most brilliant academics can be perplexed by the demands that students make of them, and that counsellors have a role in helping to unravel the confusing messages. This can be carried out in the daily contact that counsellors have with academics who consult about students who are in, or are causing, distress. It can be made more explicit when discussions about referral are entered into and where boundaries between the academic's and the counsellor's role are defined. It can be addressed through seminars and courses that focus on the teaching and tutoring relationship and where a way of thinking about work with students can be developed. All of these recognize that relationships with students are shared: that no one aspect of the college or university structure holds discrete responsibility for the psychological, or academic, development of students. Both academics and counsellors offer something that students can use at their will.

Perhaps the final comment about the therapeutic possibilities in educational life should come from a student. She had been in counselling

12   *Elsa Bell*

for some time, having been encouraged to come by concerned tutors and doctors. Teachers from school and university, and their significance as representatives of her earlier troubled relationships, were a constant theme in her counselling work. Often these relationships were perceived by her to be potentially dangerous, highly critical or overly intrusive and she struggled to find a way of holding on to her sense of herself as a separate being.

On one occasion, quite late into the work, she began to talk of a recent contact with a new tutor. This tutor had recognized her distress, and commented on it, but at the same time reminded her of the academic work that had to be addressed. The student expressed relief in counselling that the tutor had shown concern, but had kept within the boundaries of her role by reminding her of the academic task. She said, 'This is one of the best things that has happened to me in this university'.

At another time, with another student, this might have been seen by the counsellor as a comment on the relationship with her or she might have wondered whether the student was communicating that she intended to set up another, significant relationship to rival the one in the counselling room. At this point, with this student, she was able to hear the simple but important message from the student: 'Look! This tutor has offered me a relationship that has complemented the work we have been doing here. And what is more, now I can use it.'

Bibliography

Caspari, I. (1975) 'Techniques of Educational Therapy', *Association of Educational Therapy Journal*, 3(10): 1–5.

Klein, M. (1975a) 'The role of the school in the libidinal development of the child', in *Love, Guilt and Reparation and Other Works*, London: The Hogarth Press and the Institute of Psycho-Analysis. First published in 1923.

—— (1975b) 'Personification in the play of children', in *Love, Guilt and Reparation and Other Works*, London: The Hogarth Press and the Institute of Psycho-Analysis. First published in 1929.

Warburton, K. (1995) 'Student counselling: a consideration of ethical and framework issues', *Psychodynamic Counselling*, 1(3): 421–34.

Winnicott, D.W. (1971a) 'Playing: a theoretical statement', in *Playing and Reality*, Harmondsworth: Pelican.

—— (1971b) 'Case IV "Bob"', in *Therapeutic Consultations in Child Psychiatry*, London: The Hogarth Press and the Institute of Psycho-Analysis.

2 Doing clinical work in a college or university

How does the context matter?

Robert May

How shall we begin in considering the academy as a particular setting for clinical counselling? Acknowledging the importance of context, we are immediately confronted with the extraordinary variety of colleges and universities.[1] Let us look briefly at some of the obvious dimensions that matter. Working at an institution of 1,600 students will be different from working at an institution of 16,000. A smaller institution is likely to feel more manageable (at least one can usually locate the source of administrative difficulties), and to provide more of a sense of community (although the expectation that a small institution should be like a family will lead to bitter disappointment). A larger institution is less claustrophobic and likely to have a greater range of resources. It provides more room for students to make changes in their social context as their lives change. It is, for instance, my experience of a small institution that students rarely return after a psychotic episode: the anxiety and shame of confronting the same people and the same setting seems to militate against return. Clinical counselling in a largely residential institution will be different from that in a primarily 'commuter' college or university. Most obviously, the counselling and psychotherapy service[2] is likely to be called on to help with troubling events happening in the residence halls at nights and weekends. There is also likely to be a more intense peer culture in a residential institution and that will affect the experiences of students (and make the service more respectful of how the gossip circuit operates). The nature of the students themselves obviously varies widely. Issues such as the range of ages, the degree of diversity in matters of gender and ethnic background, and the question of what kind of students this institution aims to choose, all have an obvious impact on the counselling and psychotherapy service. And we must not neglect the degree of financial pressure under which a particular institution labours: questions of staffing and funding obviously bear directly on what the service can offer.

A crucial issue for the counselling and psychotherapy service is where the relevant power lies. The ultimate financial power may lie well outside of the institution, as in large national education systems or public universities dependent on funding from a state legislature. The counselling services provided to the students will probably be part of some larger department, either a health service (which may have its own complex bureaucracy) or a student services office. The particular role of a counselling and psychotherapy service cannot be properly understood without knowing to whom the service reports. The institutional context will also shape the answers to two critical questions which confront any student counselling service: how do we make our work known? How are students' voices heard? Much of what follows will circle around these two questions.

Basic functions

What does a college or university want from a counselling and psychotherapy service? It is too easy for us to assume that we have been hired to do the job we have been trained to do. But the institutional task is not necessarily the same as our own professional sense of the proper work. In the most general terms, the college or university values our work in so far as we appear to support the education, and successful graduation, of students. In a recent self-description of my institution appears the following: 'Student services at Amherst have as their primary mission facilitating, complementing, and enhancing the instruction of students at the College.' Notice two things here: we are facilitating, complementing, and enhancing, rather than doing the thing itself. And the thing itself is *instruction*; not awareness, experience, health or the like. It is a basic political reality that we counsellors and psychotherapists are not central to the institutional business of a college or university. Add to that fact the degree to which we function professionally behind closed doors and it becomes apparent that how we define and publicize our work may be crucial to our survival. For most counsellors and psychotherapists this presents challenges in the areas of politics and public relations, areas which may well not be our forte.

There are three threads running through the usual self-definition of a counselling and psychotherapy service in a college or university, the particular combination and weave depending on the particular institution. One primary task is to heal the wounded among the student body. It is my experience that a college or university always notices and values the counselling service when it comes to coping with emergencies and helping students who are radically unable to function in their work. To the extent that we are available to cope with emergencies, we help the institution contain the inevitable anxieties about insanity or suicide. In these extreme situations we will be seen as being useful in protecting the institution from blame, as protecting staff members from the potentially overwhelming anxiety of feeling responsible for very troubled students, and as having a crucial role in protecting students from harming themselves or others (in many locales, such as where I work, the legal obligation to protect against harm is part of being licensed to practise in the various mental health specialities). Counsellors located within a health service are especially likely to emphasize the language of cure, of prevention, of health and illness. Most colleges and universities will respect that rationale to some degree, but as it moves beyond issues clearly relevant to the student's capacity to function as a student, support may wear thin. Colleges and universities are not therapeutic institutions. Particularly in times of scarcity, resources will increasingly be limited to services that directly support the instructional function.[3]

There are dangers in a service becoming too identified with the 'sick' or damaged. To the extent that we represent disorder and dysfunction in the institutional mind, we will be split off and held at a distance. I am reminded of a meeting of student services personnel called together to discuss a major capital fund drive for the college. The discussion was about how to represent student services in a way that would reflect positively on the college and incline grateful graduates to open their wallets. Early on it was stated, and repeatedly seconded, that we must be very careful *not* to seem to represent the 'casualty ward', but rather to describe ourselves as in the business of helping strong and talented students do even better. The irony is that any community needs a 'casualty ward'. But that does not mean that people necessarily want to think about it. It is there for the unfortunate or disabled, not for 'us'. A college or university psychotherapy service has to contend both with the stigma attaching to the idea of psychic distress or disability and with the principled view of various articulate and respected professors that clinical counselling is at best irrelevant to the proper work of the academy, while at worst perhaps even pernicious (coddling students, creating a language of excuses for not doing one's work).

A second thread of self-definition has to do with promoting the psychological aspects of education. In the days before financial pressures became severe in higher education, this idea was given wide credence. It was generally granted, especially during the 1960s and 1970s in the USA, that education was incomplete if it focused solely on the intellectual. Students needed to know themselves and to be enlightened about human emotions, as well as about history and calculus. But this rationale has proven to lack staying power in an era of scarce resources. Education which does not show up on the transcript of course credits may be deemed of little value. Counselling services located within departments of psychology, and therefore able to offer courses for credit, have an advantage here. But increasing academic specialization has made most college and university psychology departments quite uninterested in clinical matters. There are certain kinds of 'psychoeducation' or 'health education' which do seem to bear directly on troubling behaviours in a residential college and therefore command continuing support. I mean here such things as educational programmes about sex, drugs, alcohol and eating disorders. Likewise there is support for programmes aimed directly at improving students' skills in writing and studying (we have found, for instance, that a workshop on 'Getting your work done' is one of our most popular public offerings).

The third way an institution may value us has to do with our capacity and willingness to work with the social system. It is important that the service be available for a wide range of consultations. A professor (tutor) concerned about a student persistently unable to learn, a health service clinician puzzled by a student who repeatedly comes in with vague and medically unfounded physical complaints but perhaps is depressed, a religious advisor troubled by the naive and disruptive social behaviour of one of the members of the Christian Association, or residence hall staff coping with an unidentified student vomiting repeatedly in the communal bathroom or a student repeatedly alluding to suicide in a way that alarms other students; all these are situations in which we can be helpful. We are not only available as a place to which troubling students may be referred, but also try to help those who are coping with the local social consequences of troubling behaviour. While this kind of activity requires constant alertness to ensure that it does not conflict with the individual clinical work, it has the crucial function of connecting us with a wide range of other people in the institution and of establishing our presence outside the consulting room.

Basic necessities

What is the basic institutional provision necessary for a college or university counselling and psychotherapy service? There needs to be an adequately defined task and resources sufficient to carry it out. This would include a physical space which is centrally located (not split off in some far corner of the institution) yet adequately private, and comfortable enough to be welcoming for students, not to say tolerable for the staff who will spend most of their day sitting in one place. There needs to be someone minding the physical boundary of the consultation rooms. Without a secretary or receptionist, the appointment-making process will be discouragingly haphazard and the individual clinician in his or her office will be forever distracted by real or imagined noises in the waiting room or the muted ringing of the telephone. There needs to be adequate staffing[4] and enough stability so that the staff can settle into working with each other and come to know the institution. If this basic provision is not in place then that is where the struggle and the work must be, to get the institution to honour the service enough to support it in these ways.

Necessary maintenance

This brings us to the next major issue: how do we cultivate and maintain support for the counselling and psychotherapy service? Counsellors are not necessarily adept at public relations. Our ranks probably contain more than the average number of introspective, even melancholic, temperaments. We tend to be most comfortable talking seriously with one person. Although we can cobble together a cocktail party persona when the occasion demands, it often is rather a strain. So we may tend to overlook the constant necessity of managing our boundaries with the institution. A service that operates like an encapsulated private practice, with practitioners solely dedicated to the clinical work, is not only missing chances to be of use to students but is also putting itself politically at risk.

I would like to mention some particular ways of making ourselves known, within the three general areas of value to the institution mentioned above, which my colleagues and I developed as part of our passage through a time of intense criticism and political difficulty. Direct attempts at publicity may go against the grain for counsellors, attuned as we are to the virtues of privacy and the unique qualities of face-to-face interactions. And we may be unused to the kind of critical examination that is taken for granted in academic institutions. When I first came to my current job, some twenty-five years ago, I decided to do a report at the end of the year and send it to the president. I was a bit taken aback when the president, a man whose primary career had been as a teacher, took a red pencil to my report! I decided (wrongly) that calling attention to the counselling centre was simply provoking more trouble than it was worth.

More recently I have come to value an annual report which is put together with considerable attention and then distributed widely in the institution as a way of informing people about what we do. We are careful to gather and present in this report data which bear on areas of particular concern in the institution at the moment. At Amherst, for instance, it has been important to be able to show that students of colour and gay and lesbian students are not underrepresented in the counselling centre clientele. And we try to develop special programmes in areas of current concern. In some instances the public relations value of these programmes clearly outweighs any clinical function. For instance, everyone at Amherst believes that it is very useful to have a wide range of groups available for students. At the same time our repeated experience is that students do not come to groups. We think this has to do primarily with the smallness of our institution (1,600 students on a compact residential campus) and the resultant concerns about privacy. In any case, we find ways to continue to offer a range of groups and workshops and we make sure that there is at least one descriptive mailing to the whole student body, and relevant staff in other departments, each year. There is probably a general institutional benefit in people knowing that needs are attended to and resources available. But the crucial point for us is that we will be vulnerable to criticism if we are not seen to be offering things that are generally considered useful.

For almost two decades I had employed an evaluation form given at the end of the year to students seen in the counselling centre. It was an open-ended form, with a few general questions and a lot of space for students to reflect on their experience in counselling. We learned interesting things from the responses. It served as a healthy reminder that the counsellor's retrospective view of the relationship may not always match the student's. But when it came to having to defend publically the adequacy of our services, the low percentage return on our questionnaires was deemed inadequate evidence. A recommendation was made by an outside visiting committee that we should craft a simpler rating scale and make energetic efforts to get a larger return. We have done so. This information is now presented in our annual report and turns out to be a useful counterweight to the inevitable complaints which our administrative colleagues are likely to hear (it is, of course, the discontented students who are most often heard in other departments). Our student evaluation data allows us to present the overwhelmingly satisfied voice of the majority. This is one systematic way in which we can ensure that the voice of the students we serve is heard in the institution. Since financially pressed colleges and universities are less and less likely to support a service simply on principle, it is crucial that we take steps to make sure that positive student opinion is heard. And if there is a particularly important issue about the future of the service, it is unwise to refrain from the basic political work of mobilizing opinion from students and sympathetic staff.

I mentioned above the usefulness of a structure of consultation meetings that bring counselling centre staff together with others in the institution. A college or university counselling and psychotherapy service should plan on devoting at least 20 per cent of its time to these kinds of activities. It is not only helpful to students in the end, but it is also our primary way of counteracting the hiddenness which is part of our clinical work. It is natural enough for administrators, or medical staff, to assume that if they do not see anything going on, then nothing is. Our being regularly present with colleagues in the institution is crucial.

Coping with inevitable conflict

At the same time these activities can bring us into an area of conflict. Sooner or later our wish to maintain good collegial relationships, and to make our work publically valued, comes up against the boundaries of confidentiality. This is an inevitable tension for clinical work in a college or university setting. After all, the hiddenness and privacy of our work is not simply a fetish we therapists have. It is not just because I am shy that I do most of my office work with the door closed, while professors (tutors) habitually leave the office door open while meeting with students. The boundary of confidentiality around the consulting office is one of the basic parameters which allow us to do our particular sort of work (see May 1986). In our transactions with the institution we must constantly be redefining, sometimes renegotiating, where the line of confidentiality is drawn. One must start with a clear knowledge of the legal and professional standards in one's own discipline and locale. I work in a state (geographically that is, not just psychically) which has laws about confidentiality for licensed psychologists. Basically, any and all information gathered from a professional contact, including the fact of the contact itself, may only be divulged under two circumstances, the first being one in which the client/patient has given explicit permission to divulge, and the second being one in which the clinician's professional judgement is that there is imminent risk of injury to self or another. Given the cross-currents of institutional work, I am glad to have that shore clearly defined. At least it gives me a reference point, although it may not necessarily settle the matter as far as others are concerned. The director of a college or university counselling service will be well advised to imagine ahead of time what he or she might say if the head of the institution maintains that these 'legalisms' should be overruled by the importance of 'working together in the best interest of the student' (a phrase handily vague enough to be defined by the person using it).

One hopes, on a good day, to be consistent in where one finds the balance point between confidentiality and collegiality. But, as in any tightrope act, sometimes aesthetics must be sacrificed to survival. Let me give two contrasting examples to show the kind of sway I am talking about. There is at my institution a regular meeting between deans,[5] the Director of the counselling centre, and the Director of the health service (this get-together is colloquially referred to as the 'Deans and Doctors' meeting). The purpose of these meetings is to review campus events of joint concern and, more particularly, individual students. The emphasis ends up being on troublesome individuals, so it is not always possible to get by with generically helpful comments about the issues at hand. If I know that a student has been a public concern and is likely to come up at the meeting, I will consult with the therapist and see what permission we have for comment. Our staff works with the understanding that if a student is referred to the counselling centre by the Dean's Office, or is acting in ways that are likely to stir public alarm, then the therapist should explore with the student whether we have permission to speak with the deans (or health service personnel, although that tends to feel a bit more like a district than an international boundary). Although the head dean at these meetings understands well that asking whether we are seeing a particular student is a question we cannot answer, there are other deans who *will* ask. What I *want* to say in such instances is along the lines of: 'If it would be particularly useful for you to know whether we are seeing that student, I will be glad to check to see whether we are, and whether we have permission to speak.' Since each situation is perversely unique, I am not sure whether I have ever said exactly that. It sounds a bit too composed, perhaps even prim. It represents the firm shore I rely on but never quite reach. The experience is more one of being buffeted around by my wish to collaborate and be part of the group on the one hand and on the other by my sense of professional obligation, both to individual students and to the reputation of the service. Here is an instance:

On an early winter afternoon I am strolling briskly through the College campus, taking advantage of an open hour to seek out a cappuccino at my favourite coffee shop. As I pass the steps to the main administration building, the dean of new students is there, taking the fresh air and some nicotine, and he waves me over. He describes his concerns about a first-year student. He tells me he has heard from the residence hall adviser that this student, who acts in ways that lead other students to think that she may be depressed and suicidal, has said that the counselling centre gave her a referral to a private psychiatrist. But she lets on that she is not following up on the referral. The dean expresses his concern that this student may be 'falling through the cracks'. I tell the dean that we are quite aware of this student's difficulties, that we are actively following the situation, and that we intend to make sure she finds the professional connection she needs. The dean appears reassured by that and we part, each returning to his own addiction.

So here we have an example of a seemingly useful impromptu consultation. Why is it that I am left feeling vaguely uneasy and decide that I need to describe this conversation to the counselling centre staff person who has been working with the student in question? This encounter is an example for me of competing obligations and wishes. I take seriously my institutional role of alleviating anxiety about troubling students such as this. One of the things the institution values about our service is that we can take situations like this in hand and others can then feel relief that the situation is being managed. I am also keenly aware that this dean is a tenured member of the faculty and relatively new at this job. And the Dean's Office in recent history had been a source of criticism of the counselling centre. A political rearrangement of five years' standing has me now reporting to the Dean of Students. For all of these reasons I am keen to be helpful and want the counselling centre to be seen as doing its job.

So what is the problem? The problem, simply put, is that I do not have the student's permission to let the dean know that she has been in to see us. I do know, from a previous review in staff meeting, and from my own conversations with the residence hall adviser, that the student in question has given her therapist permission to speak to her mother and has freely told the residence hall adviser about her contacts at the counselling centre. So there is no reason to think that she is particularly touchy or secretive about these matters. Legally this is arguably a grey area, and I certainly do not advocate the practice, all too common in the United States, of living one's professional life with a lawyer always looking over one's shoulder. None the less the spectre of a malpractice suit does wonderfully concentrate the mind. It leads me to remember a story I have heard about a colleague director who acted on the natural impulse to inform parents when a student was admitted to a psychiatric hospital. The resultant complaint to the psychology licensing board, while it eventually was dismissed, must have made the better part of a year of his professional life into an absolute misery.

The laws do not always accord with our personal inclinations. As the parent of a child in university, I vividly imagine my shock and anger were I to find out many months later that my daughter had been in a psychiatric hospital and I had not been informed. But the law maintains that any person 18 or over has the right to restrict that knowledge. And aside from the law, my concern is for the reputation of the counselling centre. When I first took the job of director twenty-five years ago there was a story circulating in the student gossip mill that if you went to the counselling centre the person you were talking to might pick up the phone to call a dean and announce that you were leaving school. Whatever that rumour might have been based on, it was a disaster for the reputation of the service in a small institution. So after my pleasant chat with this dean I have to worry about the (unlikely) possibility that he might in some conversation with the student indicate that he knows we are persisting in trying to work out a referral for her, and that she would then become aware that a dean has learned something about her contact at the counselling centre which she did not herself convey.

This already rather extended unpacking of the issues for me in this simple interaction deals only with the most obvious and conscious issues. I hope it does convey some of the conflicting currents through which one must find a way. It is useful to have procedures within the service which can protect counsellors from being put in uncomfortable spots too often. For instance, our secretary knows that any calls coming in for information or conversation about a particular student we are seeing, whether the call be from tutor, dean or parent, are to be directed to a staff member who is not seeing that student. This staff person's job is to try to be helpful with the concerns of the caller. The staff member will use his or her judgement in deciding whether any information needs to be conveyed to the therapist. At a minimum the therapist will be made aware of the call and can pursue the matter with the student and see whether the student wishes the therapist to be available to speak directly. This is one of the ways that we as a group carry out our wish to protect the boundary around the counselling sessions.

At the same time it is important not to protect too much. In many instances it can be helpful for the therapist to have, with permission, contact with other important people in the student's life. And there are times when the urgent needs of colleagues in other departments must take precedence over the sanctity of the session. Our staff group recently had occasion to confront this issue after an unfortunate incident in which a staff person who was in the office but not officially on duty told our secretary not to interrupt the therapist who was on duty but in a session. The result of this was that a dean was left sitting with a potentially suicidal student for considerably longer than the dean thought was right, let alone comfortable. The staff person's wish had been to 'protect' the therapist in session, but the result was a failure of our obligations toward the dean. We as a group had to reaffirm that sessions are to be interrupted if an urgent call comes in.

Summing up

Institutional life involves the repeated management of projections, counter-projections and projective identifications. For those of us who were trained primarily as individual psychotherapists, this can be a foreign and sometimes difficult work. Especially since one often has to operate unsure of the boundaries of the relevant group (who exactly is involved in a particular institutional tangle), and one can't help having the low-level anxiety that one's job is potentially at stake. We must accept that part of our work is to contain, metabolize and then feed back in a useful way the various anxieties or feelings of anger stirred up by troubling students. It is an important rule to follow up on the times when consultation with deans or tutors seems not to go well. It is crucial to stay with the anger and frustration that the others in the institution may feel when we as clinicians do not act the way they want us to (such as in the instance of wanting us immediately to banish a student who is stirring anxiety). It is important then to use the already established consultation structures to review these incidents and re-establish a sense of working together across the boundaries between the counselling service and other parts of the institution.

I do not doubt that any one of the situations I have described could be found in other counselling settings. Perhaps it is mostly the fact that I have spent all of my post-training professional years in a college setting that leads me to see it as distinct. But so it seems to me, especially when one adds in other elements which I do not have the space to treat in detail here but which receive attention in other chapters of this book. I have in mind: the way in which both the academic schedule and the developmental stage of students makes brief treatment particularly appropriate; the way in which the intellectual inclination of students means that conversation which might be seen as 'intellectualized' in the clinic is perfectly appropriate in our setting; the ways in which issues of leaving and returning are central to both the students' developmental stage and to the process of the institution (and this often means that a student's primary attachment may be to the institution and the service rather than to a particular counsellor); the ways in which a college or university's focus on diversity will be reflected in the caseload and should be reflected in the staffing of a counselling service; the way in which useful clinical technique runs the gamut from the educational, through the cognitive-behavioural, to the focal psychodynamic, and always with some provision for appropriate psychopharmacology.

There is much to be valued in doing clinical work in a college or university. It can seem alien to those fresh from the clinic (see the wonderful description by Noonan 1986) but those of us who stick it out have found things to love in the values and customs of academic institutions. On a good day the institution supports aspects of life we ourselves admire, such as learning, thoughtfulness and concern for civility, and we have the remarkable privilege of working with lively and talented students, for most of whom productive change is a real possibility. The college and

24   Robert May

university context may not be the best place for a counsellor who needs to feel central and appreciated in the institution. Those who are particularly skilful and charming may achieve that, but structurally the odds are against it. Yet, in the realm of reasonable expectations reasonably fulfilled, there is much gratification to be had from the work with both students and colleagues.

Notes

1 I have had just enough experience in the British context to know that some of the words I am using will likely have different meanings for the reader there. For instance, 'college' as I use it refers to an institution that is just as academically demanding as a university and differs only in being smaller and having no graduate or professional programmes (the undergraduate course in the United States is typically four years, beginning at age 18). I will try to be aware of other words which read radically differently on each side of the Atlantic, but can only apologize for the ones which I miss. For those interested in the United States literature on these matters, I recommend Grayson and Cauley (1989), Hanfmann (1978), May (1988) and *The Journal of College Student Psychotherapy* (Haworth Press).
2 The term 'counselling and psychotherapy service' best captures for me the range of work we do. I do not wish to get into the political and professional thicket of distinguishing between counselling and psychotherapy. College services operate within a range on that continuum. The particular qualities of a given service will be influenced by its particular institutional context: e.g., services within a health centre tend to emphasize 'treatment' whereas services outside the health service are more likely to emphasize 'normal' development, vocational services and the like.
3 Jacques Barzun, noted philosopher, historian and writer on education, was recently quoted as follows:

> College faculties and administrators have exacerbated the present cost problem by losing sight of their priorities. We have to strip higher education down to the basics – students, teachers and blackboards. Cut out all these counseling programs, opportunities for acting, student periodicals and guest lecturers. These things are in themselves valuable, but if we can't afford them, they are the things that should go, together with the personnel that operates them.
>
> (*New York Times*, 4 January 1998, Section 4A: 44)

4 What is adequate staffing? As with so many matters, there is tremendous variation here. Smaller institutions tend to have a higher staff per student ratio than larger institutions. Colleges and universities in the United States tend to have higher staffing ratios than in Great Britain. The eighteen private, selective colleges in whose statistical survey Amherst participates, have a median ratio of 1 campus mental health professional for every 520 students (the range goes from 1 per 113 to 1 per 1,583). The six universities participating in the same group have a median staff ratio of 1 per 950 students (with a range of 1 per 800 to 1 per 1,960).

5 'Deans' in the United States context are officers of the college. They are responsible for administration of the academic rules set down by the faculty, for the boundaries of entrance and exit from the institution (admission, graduation or dismissal), and for student services and student residential life. Their jobs involve a varying mixture of representing authority to students and providing support and personal counselling.

Bibliography

Grayson, P. and Cauley, K. (1989) *College Psychotherapy*, London: Guilford Press.

Hanfmann, E. (1978) *Effective Therapy for College Students*, San Francisco: Jossey-Bass.

May, R. (1986) 'Boundaries and voices in college psychotherapy', *Journal of College Student Psychotherapy*, 1: 3–28.

—— (1988) *Psychoanalytic Psychotherapy in a College Context*, New York: Praeger.

Noonan, E. (1986) 'The impact of the institution on psychotherapy', *Psychoanalytic Psychotherapy*, 2:121–30.

3   Cycles in the mind

Clinical technique and the educational cycle

Ann E. Heyno

A political slogan of the late 1990s reads 'No one forgets a good teacher'. This poster clearly shows how strongly we believe in the importance of the relationship between teachers and students. Yet despite this knowledge, the psychological impact of this relationship is rarely discussed in its own right. The emotional experience of being a student is equally well known about yet it too is largely ignored as a significant influence on the mind of the student. Despite 'knowledge' to the contrary, learning is too often thought about as a cognitive activity, split off from the emotional life of the person.

In this chapter, I will be looking at ways in which the overall educational experience, which I will call the educational cycle, has a subtle but significant impact on the mind of the student. I will demonstrate how important it is for student counsellors to allow themselves to know about the impact of the student experience on the minds of their students and also for them to know about the interrelatedness between the intellect and the emotions.

When small children start school, they normally face their first ending and their first beginning simultaneously. The ending is that of the exclusive relationship with their mother or primary carer, the beginning is the beginning of a whole new life outside the home. The way they are able to manage this transition, with all the mixed emotions it involves, will largely depend on the way they have managed earlier separations. It will also be influenced by the way in which parents and teachers are able to help them manage the excitement and anxiety of the new situation. If the emotions surrounding the transition are too great, the child may find it difficult to learn. Equally, if the child is unprepared for nursery or school, the shock may be too big to manage and the child may protest by refusing to go to school. Each time an older student enters a new educational institution, something of this earlier experience will be there in the back of his mind.

The relationship between children and their teachers is influenced by the relationship between the child and its parents. Again, the way both parties manage this will affect the way in which a child's mind is free to learn. Early learning experiences, such as the first test and how this is managed by teachers and seen by children, will affect the child's approach to being assessed. Gradually, over the years, children will gather inside them an inner experience of being a pupil and relating to teachers. They will carry this with them into further and higher education. Their expectations and fears of this more sophisticated educational experience will be coloured by their less sophisticated and childhood experience of the earlier learning process. These experiences and feelings will be projected onto their current educational experience. In this chapter, I will show how the internal educational experience of the student affects and is affected by the stages a student goes through during the academic process.

The educational cycle

Understanding the meaning of a student's presenting problems and how these might relate to his or her internal and external world is at the core of all good counselling. However, as I have indicated, in student counselling it is also important to hold in mind the specific context, the educational cycle, in which the student is experiencing these difficulties. The educational cycle is best described as the educational stages students go through as they progress within the education system. At college and university, this includes starting a course, progressing through the course, being assessed and leaving the course.

The way in which the educational cycle influences the student has its parallels in the way the stages of human development subtly affect an individual's emotions. For example, adolescents go through a stage in which they are overwhelmed by the onset of puberty and the physical changes this involves. They may not be consciously aware that these changes are affecting them and they may present for counselling with seemingly unrelated problems. However, some appreciation of the psychological impact of adolescence can help the counsellor to have a clearer picture of what might be going on for the individual and it can also put the level of anxiety attached to the presenting problem into some perspective. Ignoring or missing the relevance of this developmental stage might also mean missing the significance of its subtle effect on the feelings and behaviour of the adolescent. The same is true of missing the significance of the impact of the educational cycle on the student.

In popular psychology the impact of certain events on the emotional life of an individual is well understood. For example, unemployment, marriage, divorce, moving house, bereavement and the birth of a first child are all recognized as major stress factors, which affect everyone to some extent. It is also well accepted that some people break down under the stress of these significant life events. The effect that the educational cycle has on the minds of students is comparable with the effect that these major life events can have on all of us. The stage a student has reached on their course, or the educational pressures they are under, may provide a vital clue to the underlying reasons for the problems they are presenting. However, just as the person moving house may not be aware of the emotional upheaval this is causing them, so the student may not be consciously aware of the effect that the educational cycle is having on his emotions. For example, few students who present for counselling just before exams come complaining directly about exam anxiety. Many come in a state of acute anxiety about anything but the exams. At this time of year, there are normally a disproportionate number of students coming for counselling because of the break-up of a relationship, an unwanted pregnancy or a severe panic attack which is seemingly unrelated to the exams. For some students, the particular stage they have reached in the educational cycle may be so anxiety-provoking that they are unable to express their anxiety directly. If the anxiety cannot be expressed in words, it will be expressed indirectly, either in the form of symptoms which do not seem to have an obvious cause, or in behaviour that is difficult for the observer to understand in terms of its meaning. For some students, the pressure of studying in itself causes so much anxiety that it stirs up psychological or psychiatric difficulties which may not have surfaced under less pressured circumstances.

An example of someone who was quite out of touch with the severity of her educational anxiety was the mature student who came to the university counselling service at the beginning of May. She arrived in a state which indicated that she might be close to having a psychotic breakdown. She was shouting so loudly in the counselling room that she could be heard right down the corridor. The version of the story she was trying to tell made little sense to the counsellor except that she was saying she was going to withdraw from her course. The student was in a highly agitated state and her outbursts were punctuated with heavy sobbing. She had a history of mental illness but so far she had coped very well with the first year of her course. The counsellor was unsure how best to understand the student's distress until she thought about the fact that the first year examinations were approaching. She tentatively suggested to the student that there might be a link between her considering withdrawal at this point and anxiety about the forthcoming examinations. The suggestion brought a great sense of relief to the student who was then able to talk about her considerable academic worries in such a way that further threat of a psychotic breakdown seemed unlikely.

This brief example demonstrates how a normal part of the academic process, namely the approach of exams, can impact on an individual's emotional well-being. The forthcoming exams were not the cause of the student's severe emotional distress but they were the trigger for it. If the counsellor had not been holding the educational cycle in mind while seeing the student, she might have missed its significance. The student might have left feeling more disturbed than when she came, because her underlying anxieties had not been understood. As it was, the counsellor and the student were able to think together about the impact of the exams, so that the student could manage her emotions in such a way that they no longer interfered excessively with the learning process.

Holding in mind the stage a student has reached in the educational cycle is particularly useful, either at the time a student presents for counselling, or at a point in the counselling when what the student is saying or doing doesn't quite make sense to the counsellor. At these times, a student counsellor needs to ask the question: why is a student coming for help now? How might the stage a student has reached in their course be affecting the way they are feeling? It is also important for student counsellors to remind themselves that they are not working in isolation. Student counselling is part of a wider educational process. People who come for counselling within an educational setting, very often do so because they see their difficulties as being relevant to or linked with the educational process in some way.

Being a student

In many ways the experience of being a student is a highly stressful and complicated one. As well as being an intellectual activity, the process of learning, producing written work and being assessed is a highly emotional experience. Joining, leaving and being part of an educational institution also bring to the surface issues to do with attachment and separation. If students have unresolved difficulties in relation to these issues, then being a student is likely to bring the issues to a head and interfere with the learning process. As I have already indicated, the experience of being a student can muddy the psychological waters in a way less stressful experiences tend not to do. For most students, the experience also comes at a time in late adolescence when they have to deal with the developmental tasks of growing up and leaving home. Even mature students can return to education with the hidden agenda of completing a developmental task. Managing this task at the same time as engaging in the creative process of learning can be difficult. The majority of students do this well enough and good enough learning takes place alongside good enough personal development. For others, it is a painful experience with many psychological pitfalls, which affect development and learning.

Managing anxiety

In colleges and universities where the teaching and tutoring staff have an intuitive understanding of the stresses and strains of the learning process, many of the detrimental effects are nipped in the bud. Through its organization and structures and through good teaching, a great deal of anxiety can be contained and the basis for a good learning experience can take place. If these structures are not in place and academic staff do not have an awareness of the importance of containing their student's anxieties, then acting out in the form of dropout and underachievement can occur.

At this point I would like to introduce Wilfred Bion's notion of containment. Bion suggested that the infant communicates its strong and often stressful feelings to its mother in such a way that the mother feels the full impact of those feelings as if they were her own. Because she normally has greater emotional maturity than her child, she is able to process these feelings in her mind, think about them and communicate back to her infant that she has understood them and that they are manageable. Most mothers have this capacity, which Bion calls reverie. This intuitive interaction between mother and infant is happening whenever an infant screams and the mother manages to think about what the matter might be and calm the baby down. Bion said that this act of containment was the basis of thinking. Initially the mother thinks for the child and gradually, over time, the infant is able to take in this experience of thinking about his feelings and think for himself. Like Bion's mothers, good teachers and tutors are able intuitively to contain their students' anxieties. Their experience of the learning process enables them to communicate to the student that eventually they will be able to understand a particular theory or write a good essay or overcome overwhelming anxiety about examinations. By giving additional support to students when they first arrive in an institution, they are also able to contain anxiety about attachment and help alleviate feelings of strangeness and uncertainty. Things go wrong when containment, in Bion's sense of the term, breaks down. I will now move on to look in greater detail at how the educational cycle impacts on the learning and developmental process.

Aspects of the educational cycle

Beginnings and separations

Starting at university or college is a potential crisis point for most students. It is bound to stir up feelings about similar beginnings, such as starting at primary or secondary school. As I have said, the way it is handled by teachers and tutors can help to contain some of the potential problems. However, some students may need counselling to help them settle in or to get started on the business of being a student.

If students have difficulty with forming attachments, they may also have difficulty attaching to their course. One such student was a woman in her forties who seemed very able at interview and had excellent references from the access course she had done prior to entering university. For the first few weeks, her work was up to standard but very soon it deteriorated dramatically. Her attendance also began to drop off and she did not seem to be engaging with the course at all. At the end of the first term, her tutor was so concerned about her that she tackled the student about her attendance and the standard of her work. The student was unable to produce any explanation. The tutor noticed that the student also appeared to be depressed, so suggested that she might find it easier to explore her difficulties with a counsellor. In counselling it became clear that the student had marital and financial problems which she feared would prevent her from completing the course. She was so worried about this that she could not think about it, or allow herself to achieve anything. Instead of being able to talk about the problem, she was acting it out in the form of poor performance and poor attendance. It also transpired that the student had a recent history of relationships that had not worked out and she was terrified of committing herself to anyone or anything, however much she wanted to. As a small child, she had spent a considerable amount of time in hospital following an accident in which she had almost died. Her parents had been so upset by what had happened that they found it difficult to help her with the feelings aroused by the hospital separations.

For this student, her academic problem in properly attaching to her course was closely linked to her difficulties in forming attachments and her fear of subsequent separations. The discrepancy between her obvious potential and her weak performance provided me with a clue that something was seriously wrong. Because the problem was occurring at the beginning of a student's course, it was useful to follow the train of thought that led to a possible link between poor performance and difficulties attaching to the course. She had managed to settle into the access course because the group had been small and she had had a great deal of contact and support from the tutors. When she entered university she felt more alone in a larger group and in a setting which required more independence from its students.

Beginnings as a trigger

In addition to issues so directly linked to attachment, starting a course can stir up difficulties that may have been dormant until that point. The anxiety surrounding joining a new educational institution can bring other difficulties into the foreground. Take, for example, the student who came to the counselling service in the third week of her first term, complaining of not being able to study. She said she had not yet enrolled on the course and was uncertain whether she should. She was finding London rather noisy and crowded and was not sure whether she liked the course. At one level her problem could have been put down to homesickness but that would have been to simplify the issue. After several counselling sessions, it emerged that the student's mother had recently been made redundant. The student, who was studying the same subject as her mother, was feeling guilty about succeeding in an area in which she perceived her mother to have failed. The impact of starting the course had stirred up her anxieties and rivalries in relation to her mother and at the point of coming for help she was in danger of ruining her own academic career to deal with her guilt and rivalry towards her mother.

Another student for whom starting university proved to be the catalyst for unresolved family issues was 19-year-old Clare. She was referred for counselling by the college doctor in the middle of the first term of her first year because she was having difficulty sleeping. At our first meeting, she told me she wanted help before her problem turned into a crisis. Her difficulties had started when she was 17 and her mother had left home to live with another man. In Clare's mind, the family had been perfect until that moment. As the youngest of three sisters, she was to have been the last to leave home and go to university and she was very much looking forward to this. Her mother was a teacher and had always encouraged her children to achieve academically. She left home a few months before Clare's 'A' levels but nevertheless Clare worked hard and achieved good grades.

In our first few meetings, she spoke very movingly about her 'ideal family' and how the dream had been shattered by her mother's departure. She told me that soon after her mother left, her father decided they should move to a small flat. Once they had moved he began to have a series of girlfriends. The way she described his behaviour seemed more appropriate to someone of her age, rather than his. At this point, she felt as if she no longer had a family or parents. Nevertheless, she went ahead with her plans to do a degree at university and moved into the halls of residence. Her crisis came once she had settled in. She had survived the actual trauma of her family breaking up and the immediate transition from home to university but the process of starting a course had subtly evoked previously buried feelings about what had happened. For Clare, starting university acted as the trigger for feelings which had actually been around for a couple of years but which only came to the surface at the point at which she left home in a concrete way.

The students described so far were all at some risk of leaving their courses because of the difficulties stirred up by starting at university. Often students act out their feelings at this stage and turn away from education simply because they cannot see another way of resolving their emotional difficulties.

Examinations

Another potential crisis point for students is the examination period. As I have already indicated, this may also produce behaviour and symptoms that may not be immediately associated with anxiety about assessment. At the university counselling service where I work, we are always inundated with referrals in the weeks proceeding the exam period. Every year, this surprises us because few of these students come asking directly for help with exams. Each year we are drawn into a state of panic because the volume of students coming for help feels unmanageable. Each time we forget that the situation will ease a little once the exams are over. I am now convinced that what we go through at exam time is both normal and inevitable. It has little to do with our efficiency, organization or capacity to manage our anxiety. However, each year, we make plans to organize ourselves better in the vain hope that this will take away the anxiety. Unfortunately it never does because this isn't possible. What we go through each exam time has its parallel in what the students are going through. What we experience, as student counsellors, in the period leading up to the exams, is part of the process described by Bion in his theory of containment. The students, who also seem to forget or deny to themselves that the exams are looming, project their unmanageable anxiety into the counselling service and the counsellors absorb and experience this anxiety.

When students present themselves in a panic about something other than exams during this period, they may be so agitated that they are unable to think. The student counsellor's initial task is to do their thinking for them in Bion's sense of the word. What counsellors have to do is to take their student's anxiety on board and process it in their minds. They have to think to themselves: 'Is the timing of this person's anxiety relevant? Are the difficulties they are having being fuelled by such a high level of persecutory anxiety about the exams that they do not feel they have the emotional capacity to process it?' The examination panic might be so severe that it cannot be thought about and other worries are brought to the surface instead. Or it might be that the examinations and a fear of failure bring to the surface disturbance of the kind described in my first example in this chapter.

January blues

So far, I have looked at some of the ways in which entering education and facing assessment in the pre-examination period can have a subtle impact on a student's psyche. I will now move to consider other, often puzzling ways, in which the educational cycle can impact on the individual. A mature student, who came for counselling in her first year, complained of a lack of confidence and difficulty settling in. At the start of her second year, she felt sufficiently confident to stop counselling and enjoy getting on with her course. It was therefore a surprise to me when she reappeared in the January of her final year saying she was going to drop out. When I had last seen her, she was fully integrated into student life and loved her course. When she came to see me the second time round, she said she was utterly convinced that leaving university immediately was the only answer. With only two terms to go, I found this decision rather puzzling. I also wondered why she was coming to see me if she had so clearly made up her mind to leave. It took us several counselling sessions to understand what was going on. As it turned out, my student was in such a state about her course because it was about to end. Her threat to leave prematurely was an angry way of rejecting university before it rejected her. She was also struggling with anger and disappointment, laced with envy. She had come on the course after working for many years as a secretary. At work, she had always felt she could do her boss's job just as well as her boss could. Coming to university was a way of proving this to herself. As she neared the end of her three years, she realized that a degree on its own would not necessarily provide the career and status she was looking for. In her mind, she had imagined that after graduating, she would become a lecturer and spend her time going around the Third World doing lecture tours. As reality began to dawn, she felt angry and cheated. Much of her anger was directed towards me and towards her lecturers. 'It's all right for you', she said. 'You've got a job. You can stay at university. In a few month's I have got to leave.'

This student's crisis, which came in the January of her final year, is typical. There is anecdotal evidence to suggest that January is a peak time for anxiety in final year students. It may be that leaving education clashes with the well-recognized post-Christmas blues period, or it may be that it marks the point at which the end of the course seems inevitable. Like the earlier crises I have described, the triggers for January blues are rarely immediately obvious to the counsellor, which is why it is important to hold the rhythm of the educational cycle in mind when seeing students.

Leaving education

For the student who wanted to leave her course in the January of her final year, the reality of facing life after university proved to be her greatest worry. Many students who present for counselling in a crisis in the last year of their degree have similar anxieties. In *The Suicidal Adolescent*, Moses Laufer says,

> It is usually sometime in adolescence that the person will have to make decisions that will affect his whole future life, such as his future work, his future sexual partner, his future relationship to himself either as a 'successful' person or as a 'failure'. The consequences of the stresses or of the trouble can often be as serious as the trouble itself.
>
> (1995: 8)

Later in the book it is suggested that some adolescents break down when they reach the end of university because 'they may feel that the time to be an adolescent has run out'. Certainly, some of the final year students who come for counselling feel that leaving university is like having to go through a door they don't feel ready to open. In their imagination, graduating means, as Laufer suggests, that they will also have to grow up, find a partner, get a job and make a home all at once. For some, that prospect is just too daunting. A final year crisis, which often comes in the form of unexpected or uncharacteristic academic failure, can be a way of expressing anxieties that can't be verbalized directly.

One student I saw felt he would never be able to survive financially without his parents' support when he left university. To help him make the most of his studies, his parents had suggested he live at home throughout his course. They gave him all the money he needed and persuaded him not to take any paid work while he was at university. During most of his course, he studied hard and did very well academically. Then suddenly in his final term, the standard of his work dropped and he failed to meet the deadline for his final project. Instead he fell passionately in love with a much older woman on his course and shocked his parents by saying he was going to move in with her. She had a home and two small children and was in a financial position to support him while he looked for work. It was only when he eventually found a part-time job that the full impact of what he had done hit him. He realized he had jumped out of the frying pan into the fire because he had had so little faith that anyone would ever employ him and he had feared he would remain a child forever. As a self-fulfilling prophecy, he had unconsciously taken his place in the older woman's home not as her lover but as one of her children. Fortunately, the university was sympathetic to his extenuating circumstances and the examination board allowed him extra time to hand in his final project. In counselling, he was able to work on his fears about leaving university and growing up.

Another student, who found herself unable to complete her coursework or sit for her final exams, was referred to the counselling service by her tutor in a state of deep depression, weeks before she was about to leave. Until these last weeks, she had been a successful student and her tutor could not understand why she was failing now. At first, the reasons for her sudden study block made no sense to her at all. All she knew was that she felt depressed and couldn't see the point in continuing, either with her course or with her life. Her father was a successful lawyer who had always expected her to follow in his footsteps. She had gone along with this because she loved her father and felt she had no choice but to respect his wishes. Consciously she was trying to please him and do what he wanted but unconsciously she was very angry indeed. She felt trapped in an internal conflict from which she feared she would never escape. Like the student who went to live with the older woman, this student felt she would never be able emotionally to extricate herself from her father's wishes. She eventually told me she saw no point in graduating or living because she felt she would never make the quantum leap from childhood to adulthood, so what was the point finishing her course. With her doctor's support, I was able to help her through the crisis. She became more aware of her internal hostility towards her father, which had previously expressed itself in compliance. As she became more confident, she was able to stand up to him more easily and eventually took a year out to decide what she wanted to do.

The social context

The impact of the educational cycle on the mind of the student has been the subject of this chapter. Before concluding, I would like to refer to another important influence, that of the wider social and political context in which the student is studying. In the latter part of the twentieth century, young people have been subject to a highly materialistic, market-driven culture, in which personal worth is too often measured in financial terms. This emphasis on material success, coupled with a greater emphasis on skills, high levels of unemployment and job uncertainty have all played a part in orchestrating the state of students' minds. For many of them, the joy of learning has been replaced by a desire to achieve high grades at any cost. Additionally the higher divorce rate has affected young people's belief in the durability of relationships. There is a sense that nothing is certain or permanent. Alongside this there is increased depression and a higher incidence of students with suicidal thoughts. I cannot help but conclude that these and other social influences have affected young people's minds in a similar way to the processes described in this chapter on the educational cycle. It is therefore important that student counsellors bear in mind these social influences when seeing students.

In summary, I have suggested in this chapter that the educational stages which students go through during their time at college or university have a significant impact on them psychologically. Different students have varying capacities to deal with certain stress points in the educational cycle and some educational institutions are better at containing their students' anxieties than others. Student counsellors need to be constantly alert to the stages their students are going through, so that they can help them make sense of what can sometimes feel like frighteningly strong and incomprehensible feelings.

Bibliography

Bell, E. (1996) *Counselling in Further and Higher Education*, Buckingham: Open University Press.

Bion, W. (1967a) 'Attacks on linking', in *Second Thoughts*, London: Heinemann. First published in 1959.

—— (1967b) 'A theory of thinking', in *Second Thoughts*, London: Heinemann. First published in 1962.

Britton, R. (1992) 'Keeping things in mind', in *Clinical Lectures on Klein and Bion*, London: The New Library of Psychoanalysis, Routledge.

Coren, A. (1997) *A Psychodynamic Approach to Education*, London: Sheldon Press.

Klein, M. (1988) *Envy and Gratitude and Other Works 1946–1963*, London: Virago Press.

Heyno, A. (1996) 'Adhesive learning', paper given at the Association for Student Counselling conference, 'Culture and psyche in transition: a European perspective on student psychological health', Sussex University.

Laufer, M. (1995) *The Suicidal Adolescent*, London: Karnac Books.
O'Shaughnessy, E. (1981) 'W.R. Bion's theory of thinking and new techniques in child analysis', in Elizabeth Bott Spillius (ed.), *Melanie Klein Today: Developments in Theory and Practice, Volume 2: Mainly Practice*, London: The New Library of Psychoanalysis, Routledge.

4   Student empowerment, staff support and organizational stress

Suzanna Stein

Introduction

Counselling in an institution of further or higher education differs from counselling in private practice, because in a university or college the educational priorities will structure and contain the counselling experience for the student. University and college counselling is a unique, dynamic and therapeutic practice in its own right (O'Carroll 1997). This chapter will present an approach to counselling in such settings which is both pragmatic and flexible.

Pragmatism

University and college counselling is only one of many services provided to support students, and plays a relatively small, yet important, part in the life of most of these organizations. The main purpose of the counselling is to help students through periods of emotional difficulty, so that they can complete their courses. Its funding and support will continue only as long as it serves the needs of the institution. The student counselling service in a university or college should be seen as an integral part of the educational programme, complementary to teaching (Bell 1996). It may be a personal disaster for the student who breaks down halfway through a course, and as a consequence withdraws. For the institution, a withdrawal will represent a significant financial loss, which in the present climate is quite serious. A counselling service gains credibility from academic departments if it can demonstrate an ability to retain students who, without help, might otherwise have left (Stein 1997a).

Elsa Bell (1996) has chronicled the development of student counselling in further and higher education. It is generally accepted that emotional factors can detrimentally affect learning and that their alleviation is desirable (Malleson 1963; Salzberger-Wittenberg 1983). For example, in a recent study at the University of Birmingham (Rickinson 1997) a group of final year undergraduates who consulted the counselling service were divided into two groups – those who received four to six sessions of counselling compared to a matched control group who did not. Those who received counselling showed a large fall in measures of anxiety four weeks later, in comparison with the control group, where there were negligible changes in anxiety levels. Although final degree outcome was not influenced, the short-term reduction in anxiety levels achieved through the counselling enabled students to complete their education with markedly less distress. As well as helping with individual students the university counsellor also has an important role in the planning of better pastoral care provision in the institution.

Flexibility

University and college counselling is by definition pragmatic and so will embrace a pluralistic model using several different schools of therapy. Samuels (1997) suggests a counselling approach which should reconcile the world of therapy with the real social and economic difficulties which confront the student. Many counsellors working in an educational setting will already work with this approach, moving the focus of therapy flexibly; at times working through the traumas of the past, such as child abuse or loss, while at other times focusing more on the issues of current concern.

Presenting problems vary widely. Some students will have intense personal concerns which adversely affect their ability to study. Others may pursue study to the exclusion of a normal lifestyle and so become depressed and even suicidal (Heyno 1997). Many students will experience financial poverty, while a few students will lack the necessary social skills to survive communal living and so become angry or upset. The counsellor has a role in clarifying with the student more precisely what the underlying difficulty is before an appropriate remedy is sought.

University counselling based on the Egan model

There are many different types of psychotherapy, such as the psychodynamic, cognitive-behavioural or client-centred approaches. An integrative therapeutic model is becoming increasingly popular as it combines the best practice of the main counselling philosophies, but this may inevitably result in a dilution of particular theoretical models.

In the context of brief psychotherapeutic work many counsellors have adopted the Egan model which is both flexible and pragmatic and appears to be particularly helpful for brief work (4–6 sessions) in an educational setting (Stein 1991). In support of this, Rickinson (1997: 282–3) writes:

In my clinical experience I have been impressed by the capacity of undergraduates to use very brief counselling interventions to rework earlier unresolved developmental conflicts, gain insight and self understanding, and by internalising the counselling process develop the capacity to counsel themselves. The same process may take much longer with adults over 25 years of age or in a different context.

The Egan model is a three-stage problem-solving model, which gives helpers the 'technology of helping' (Egan 1990: 409). It is a 'stand alone' model (Egan 1990: v) yet its principles and methods can be incorporated into other approaches to helping.

Stage 1 'The present scenario' helps clients to identify, explore and clarify their problems and unused opportunities. Egan (1990) feels that, to empower the client, problems can paradoxically be turned into opportunities. As one manages a situation better, one gains a sense of relief and control over one's life. 'Blind spots' will need to be challenged, so that a more realistic and creative way of looking at life can be facilitated. This is 'one of the major ways in which counsellors can empower clients' (Egan 1990: 34). Leverage is then sought, and the client's commitment to work on issues in the counselling that will make a difference.

Stage 2 'Developing a preferred scenario' helps the client to develop a range of possibilities for a better future. Egan (1994) uses future-orientated questions and probes to help 'clients invent the future' (Egan 1994: 245).

Stage 3 'Getting there' offers support to the client while considering various strategies that will achieve the desired goal. If there are sub-goals, then each will have its own set of strategies. Effective counsellors will help the client to foresee difficulties, 'the Shadow Side' that might arise during the actual carrying out of their plans. Egan insists that evaluation of progress needs to be considered at every stage of the helping process and that a successful outcome to the counselling interaction is when the client is managing life better. One might also add 'improved academic learning' as a desired goal of counselling in the university or college context, which may not be explicitly stated, but is often the outcome after counselling. The student will feel happier and less distressed, when problems or feelings are contained and managed, so that mental energy can be used where it belongs – in new learning, rather than dwelling on old and unresolved conflicts.

A good therapeutic relationship is essential for a successful outcome and the essential ingredients for such a therapeutic relationship are well described by Carl Rogers (1957), as involving empathy, positive regard, genuineness and non-judgementalism. If the person being helped perceives the relationship as one wherein the therapist desires to understand there is a good chance of a successful outcome (Quinn 1950). Seeman (1954) found that success in psychotherapy is closely associated with a strong and growing mutual liking and respect between client and therapist. More recently, Clarkson (1995) has documented five different kinds of therapeutic relationship which span all approaches:

- the working alliance;
- the transference/counter-transference;
- the developmentally needed or reparative;
- the person-to-person;
- the transpersonal.

The following case study will illustrate an integrative, Egan-based, brief focused counselling approach for a student presenting in a crisis with a complex relationship difficulty.

Meena was a 22-year-old Asian student on a one-year postgraduate course in education. Pretty and intense, she presented with a relationship problem. She was in love with an English/Caucasian psychologist who seemed to be leading her a merry dance. Basic Rogerian principles were used to establish a warm and trusting relationship, which included the counsellor checking with the client that she felt comfortable with a non-Asian counsellor. In the sessions, personal boundaries soon became important, since her boyfriend appeared to be abusing the relationship. He was structuring a pseudo-therapeutic-type relationship with her, probing intensively into her relationship with her parents, her previous sexual partners and asking her to work on her 'problems' with him. He had 'diagnosed' her as needing psychological help and insisted that, as she was not 'improving', she should seek help from her GP. He claimed that her 'problems' were interfering with their relationship. The problems were indeed coming to a head as she wanted him to commit to the relationship while he on the other hand was ambivalent and somewhat distant. He enjoyed sex with her, as she did with him, and yet he had recently applied to Australia for an overseas placement of one year's duration. As the interview for his placement drew nearer, she felt increasingly 'used' as a sexual object and was becoming frigid and cold towards him. He persistently refused to talk to her about any long-term future between them.

Meena's work on the course deteriorated, as she was often preoccupied, feeling at times tearful and suicidal. She realized how important the course was to her, since successful completion would help her reach economic independence from a loving but overprotective family that did not set great store in her teaching aspirations. Her father would have preferred her not to have a career, but to settle down in an approved Asian marriage.

Using the Egan model, the future-orientated questions of Stage 2 involved her deciding on what constituted a satisfactory relationship with her boyfriend, while Stage 3 looked at changing her behaviour and assumptions.

During the counselling it was clear that her six sessions would need some focus and that there would be insufficient time to explore, at a leisurely pace, her relationship with her parents, brother and sisters. There was an additional institutional pressure which also affected the type of therapy in that she was preparing for her teaching practice. This meant a placement away from the university site, and away from the counselling service, for a whole term.

Using the terminology of the Egan model, her presenting problem was clearly an unsatisfactory and potentially abusive relationship that resulted in her becoming anxious and depressed. Using brief focused counselling, we tracked this via the nightmares that she was having, to an earlier experience of being sexually abused by a male cousin. This led to broken boundaries within herself and a lack of self-esteem which had allowed her to engage in a relationship that she found extremely problematic. Because she was also having suicidal thoughts, Meena was referred to her GP who prescribed a course of antidepressants. The counselling allowed her to explore her positive behaviours and utilize assertiveness techniques; she became more able to deal with the problem of her boyfriend's placement in Australia and his apparent lack of concern for her distress. We role-played her intended statements to her boyfriend, as well as to her father, preparing her for her role in adult life as an independent teacher and person.

Meena telephoned me three months after leaving the university. Her nightmares had stopped and her depression was relieved. Her boyfriend was writing and phoning regularly from Australia, but she felt sufficiently assertive to let things take their course. She also felt able to leave her parents' home and move in with a sibling with whom she was able to share some of her earlier difficulties with her father, as well as the earlier abuse. She was enjoying her first teaching post, had attained her independence and was looking forward to her future. Meena's empowerment was achieved through her work in the counselling as well as the treatment offered by her GP. The resources of the institution were used, and the teaching placement itself (initially viewed negatively by the client when she was depressed and struggling with her work) emerged as one of the levers for change.

Throughout the counselling my feelings of empathy and respect, and willingness to listen without judgement, served to build a warm thera-peutic relationship. Within this working alliance (Clarkson 1995), change and growth could take place.

Typical presenting problems in a university or college setting

In addition to dealing with anxiety, depression and general relationship problems, certain other problems seem to present rather more frequently in university and college counselling services: these include homesickness and exam stress, as well as difficulties in managing psychiatric illness. Staff also turn to the counselling service at times to deal with their own distress, or to seek consultation when they are worried about aspects of their students' behaviour.

Counselling for homesickness

Universities can be very stressful places, with homesickness affecting up to two-thirds of first-year residential students (Fisher 1989). In her book Dr Fisher views homesickness in the context of an adverse reaction to relocation which can result in psychological and physical ill health. Moves can create periods of stress, for they are life events characterized by loss, transition and change. Of particular significance in thinking about homesickness in a university or college counselling setting is the level of bereavement or sadness a student may feel when a loved person or environment has been left behind. Not only can health be affected but a student's thinking ability can become impaired (Fisher 1989). First-year residential students are particularly at risk, as they are in a completely new environment and are often cut off from family support through geographical distance. Students affected by homesickness may also express discontent with their academic courses and their surroundings as well as feeling a lack of commitment to the university or college in general. 'Separation anxiety' is often experienced.

It is helpful if the counselling for homesickness focuses on certain specific clinical areas. Clarkson (1995) suggests that one aspect of the therapeutic relationship is 'reparative': in this case, the therapy may provide a safe place for the discussion of what has been 'lost'. Second, it is helpful if the counselling is problem-focused, with goal- or task-setting, so that changes can take place whereby the university environment is experienced as less threatening. Possibilities such as encouraging the attendance of a social or sporting event which reflects one of the client's interests should be explored. Fisher (1989) has described how high levels of commitment result in attention which is externally dominated by the outside world and this in turn helps to keep thoughts of homesickness at bay.

Third, the counsellor should explain to the student that in cases of homesickness the distressing symptoms (depression and disorientation; loss of memory and concentration; poor health; somatization) are almost always transient, and will generally wane with the passage of time. It is also helpful for the counsellor to hold in mind theories of bereavement counselling (Parkes 1972; Stedeford 1991) as well as models of trauma counselling and psychological debriefing (Rose 1997).

At an organizational level, to minimize student distress, university and college counsellors should be involved with the induction of new students. The initial welcome address may be followed up by mid-term meetings, when students are better orientated, and less 'traumatized'. Students will be more receptive to information on the support services when their own anxieties have lessened.

Overseas students

Many universities and colleges will make special provision for overseas students who may face intense homesickness coupled with cultural and language readjustment. An international officer and other designated staff may arrange orientation programmes, group 'drop in' sessions and various cultural/recreational/social events to help students adjust to the new setting. Many universities and colleges also encourage peer support or mentoring and friendship schemes to allow the overseas student to adjust to the new 'family' of the organization. Practical as well as language support will need to be provided for some overseas students. A few overseas students may seek out the counsellor to help deal with the emotions of alienation and uprootedness. The problem is further exacerbated if the overseas student is an asylum seeker or a refugee who may need counselling support for personal traumas sustained in the country of origin and/or as a consequence of the nature of their arrival in the UK. There are specialist organisations such as UKCOSA: The Council for International Education, which can provide guidance, information and further training for counselling and advisory staff dealing with such clients. Counsellors will need at all times to be sensitive to differences in culture and race, which can have an effect on the counselling relationship and process (Lago and Thompson 1996).

Paolo, a residential first-year law student, self-referred for counselling. He was 19, Maltese and bilingual. He had always wanted to study law. He came to England partly to escape from his over-possessive parents, and to prove to his family that he could succeed academically in a rigorous discipline such as law. A shy, hesitant student, he shared his story of homesickness with me. He was away from his parents for the first time in his life and felt miserable, depressed and unable to study. The environment and the course had brought to the surface difficulties from the past. Emotionally, he had been very dependent on his parents – even sharing a bed with them until his arrival at the university. An additional factor was that the academic pressures reawakened feelings of intellectual inferiority in himself. A tutor thought he might be dyslexic as he complained of difficulties with organizing his work, taking notes and writing. He felt dejected and was beginning to have negative thoughts. Paolo was clearly not coping, desperately trying to prove to his parents and himself that he was (or ought to be) a successful student.

Using a reparative therapeutic relationship (Clarkson 1995), I tried to recreate for Paolo a safe and confidential environment where he could freely discuss his worries and depression. His need to separate from his parents was obvious, and yet his homesickness and reactive depression were arousing such strong emotions in him that he was thinking of returning home to Malta.

Because of the immediacy of the crisis, and the real possibility that he might quite abruptly decide to leave, I felt it was inappropriate to delve into a long-term therapeutic exploration of his extreme emotional closeness with his parents, although this was clearly the underlying psychopathology.

Instead, using the Egan model, the therapy focused on more practical issues such as managing the current homesickness, with its attendant feelings of depression, and organizing study skills support. It was essential for him to feel better in himself; to have contact with his father and mother; and to gain confidence in his ability to study and present his work better. The action stage (Stage 2 in the Egan model) involved arranging a dyslexia test (he was found to be dyslexic) followed by some individual tutorial support and attendance at a dyslexia study support group. He also telephoned his father and explained how miserable and homesick he was feeling. His father flew from Malta to spend three days with him in his room in halls. This greatly cheered Paolo.

Paolo had six sessions of counselling at the beginning of the first term of his first year, and he began to feel better. I still see him from time to time and he looks more confident: his depression and acute home-sickness have passed. He is working well and achieving good grades. Through the counselling Paolo improved sufficiently to continue with his studies and enjoy his stay in this country. He also benefited from the dyslexia support which he found helpful. Interestingly, on his return from Malta following each university vacation, he books in for one or two sessions of brief counselling to re-establish our reparative therapeutic relationship (Clarkson 1995), and to share with me that he is feeling a little down again and lacking in confidence. These brief sessions deal again with the bereavement and change aspect of homesickness and bear out Dr Fisher's research that homesickness or distress following transition can be re-experienced repeatedly, although each episode may become more manageable for some students. For other students the pain can remain acute (Fisher 1989).

Counselling for examination stress

Examinations and assessments are an integral part of academic life, but at the same time they can be severe stressors. High arousal and a sense of low control will actively initiate stress (Fisher 1994). Examination counselling will therefore need to be focused on techniques and strategies used for decreasing anxiety associated with learning or exams. Counselling offered for 'exam nerves' is more likely to be effective if it is also linked to learning and study skills support. A programme of revision and examination group workshops can bring benefit to many students. Such exam groups offer practical support as well as peer support, and are to be recommended. Some university and college counselling services offer complementary therapy (aromatherapy and hypnotherapy) as part of a stress management programme (Stein 1997a) or run weekly therapy groups for anxiety. There are many ways in which the counselling service, by liaising with tutors, can support students in the run-up to examinations. The counsellor, for instance, can be invited in to the academic year group, to give a talk on stress management to the whole cohort. This is particularly useful for accessing those students who would normally be reticent about approaching a counsellor. Tutors will also be referring individual students to counselling for anxieties which may have more deep-rooted causes. Cognitive-behavioural anxiety- and stress-management techniques may be preferable to longer term psychotherapy (Palmer 1997) for some students. Counselling for examination stress needs to be pragmatic and flexible in a university or college setting.

The psychiatrically ill student

In one large university or college, 6 per cent of the total population attend for counselling in any one year (Stein 1997a); within that figure, one in five students (or 1.2 per cent of the total population) will have a clinical disorder of sufficient severity to indicate a referral to a doctor, usually the GP but sometimes the psychiatrist. While these figures may seem to be high, it should be noted that rates of psychiatric disorder in the community are high. Ten per cent of the population aged 16–65 will consult a GP in any one year with a psychological/psychiatric problem or disorder. Around one in five of these (or 2 per cent of the total population) are referred on to a psychiatrist (Goldberg and Huxley 1980).

The counselling service has an important role to play in supporting these students. As with any client, the initial assessment can determine whether counselling is appropriate, and in some cases it may not be. With some psychiatrically ill students (particularly those with psychiatric distress) care must be taken to clarify whether the client has sufficient ego strength and insight to benefit from therapeutic counselling. In the presence of severe illness it may be preferable for the counsellor to offer only a supportive role, while medical or psychiatric intervention takes precedence. It is sometimes helpful, given the client's consent, if a joint therapeutic approach is adopted, involving the counsellor, the GP or psychiatrist, and/or the community psychiatric nurse. Many students can be held on their academic course with such a combined approach. Furthermore, the counselling relationship may actually facilitate the (hesitant) client's referral to the medical/psychiatric services. For the mentally ill, compliance with medical treatment is important, and the counselling service is usually in a good position to facilitate this.

A small number of students may develop serious psychotic illnesses for the first time during their university or college career. It should be noted that the age of onset for schizophrenia is often between 18 and 25, while manic depressive illnesses can also start at this time. The first episode of a major mental illness or psychotic disorder is a very frightening experience for the client, and in the presence of bizarre or suicidal behaviour will also cause great consternation in those around them. In these cases the counsellor may commonly be called in during an emergency but there is no role for 'counselling' as such. The task is to get specialized help to the student as quickly as possible and if necessary obtain psychiatric admission. This may have to be on a compulsory basis under the Mental Health Act, in which case the patient's GP, the duty social worker and the catchment area psychiatrist will be involved. The task of the counsellor in such cases is to alert the relevant medical personnel, contain the situation as best as possible until help arrives, and allay anxiety in those involved.

After such an admission the client may need a term, if not a year out, and then a return to the university or college with a managed care plan. Psychiatric or medical consultation is advisable if the counsellor offers support to more seriously psychiatrically ill students. Without such consultative support, there is a risk of inappropriate counselling being offered, and also counsellor 'burnout', while the student may also be placed in jeopardy.

Elsa Bell (1996) has described how university counselling services in the UK often work independently of the psychiatric and medical services. This is in marked contrast to the American system where these services are often interdependent and between 10 and 25 per cent of students seen for counselling in the university health centre may be on medication (Bell 1996). The split in the UK is unfortunate, and often unsupportive to the counsellor. A second factor of significance is that some counsellors still view antidepressant or antipsychotic drugs with suspicion, despite recent medical advances. There is also sometimes a distrust of the psychiatric services. A better understanding between the professions should be reached and some psychiatric training and support for counsellors could be offered at postgraduate level.

Working with the wider institutional context

The personal tutor and the counselling service

Today all university students are assigned a personal tutor whose task it is to 'track' the student's progress through the system and offer guidance, advice and support on issues impacting on the work. This primary task of the personal tutor (who is sometimes called an academic tutor or a year tutor) is not well defined, and can be open to interpretation and sometimes abuse. Some tutors will readily seek advice from the counselling staff, particularly when there are signs of emotional distress in students. Others may distance themselves completely from a pastoral role, taking an interest primarily in academic issues.

Tutors need help and information on what the counselling service can and cannot do, as well as information on dealing with the student in crisis. This is usually achieved through workshops and training, and sometimes through circulating short student services manuals specifically written for tutors (Allen 1995). It is also helpful to discuss with tutors role delineation such as whose primary task it is to offer psychological support and counselling at the time of difficulty; as well as the techniques of appropriate referral. There are still many areas of overlap between the role of the counselling service and that of the personal tutor, with some tutors being content to offer support and others becoming anxious or defensive about dealing with emotional issues.

A tutor may become so supportive to a student with emotional problems that disengagement becomes problematic, making referral on to the counsellor difficult. There is a skill in listening to and calibrating the appropriate moment when a referral may be suggested and then made. If the suggestion is made too soon in the tutorial, the student may feel rejected. If the suggestion is made too late, a dependent relationship will already have been formed. University counsellors should be aware of the dynamics of this situation and the feelings associated with referral and will need to support tutors in this task. Such support is also helpful to non-tutorial staff engaged in pastoral care, such as accommodation staff, halls managers and wardens. It should be noted that many of the students in their charge, as well as being young, may also be immature and lacking in basic life skills. Others will have come from difficult backgrounds and might seek psychological treatment regardless of the environment they are in. A brief case history is presented below to illustrate the problems of a late referral from a college tutor to the counselling service with a highly disturbed student.

A female tutor had a 'special relationship' with a tutee, taking her out to lunch, listening to her concerns, and involving herself with worrying about the tutee's emotional difficulties. The tutee was bisexual and shared with the tutor her painful history of childhood abuse and the problems of separating from a former lesbian relationship.

The tutor was beginning to feel uncomfortable and overwhelmed with the tutee's increasing academic and emotional dependency on her. The student, who was prone to depression, became very confused and in a fit of depression took an overdose. It was only at that point that I was brought in with a request to see the student.

The tutor was distressed and upset and wished the university counsellor to 'take her on for counselling' as 'it was all too much' for her. The tutor was happily married and could no longer cope with the student's emotional intensity, and semi-lesbian advances. In moving from her tutoring role into a semi-counselling role with a student who was extremely unstable, the tutor was clearly getting into difficulties.

The counselling that followed was successful in part, but during periods of academic pressure the student broke from the counselling to resume her dependent relationship with the tutor. This splitting was fairly destructive in outcome as the student felt she underachieved in her final examination and broke down, acting out her anger in abusive telephone threats to the tutor.

The counselling service in an educational institution does not sit outside, but coexists with, the educational services. A robust, personal and inter-active liaison with staff is essential so that staff have confidence in asking for advice and referring appropriately. This does not compromise client confidentiality. Staff may feel reluctant to refer a student to a counsellor they do not know – particularly if the subject matter is very sensitive.

Organizational stress

The stress caused by working in an institution can be considerable. However, not all stress is 'bad' – indeed, it may even provide additional incentive to perform better, revise or work more effectively, and devote time to the task in hand. Too much stress or pressure, however, causes problems. Sometimes the demand may exceed the capacity to perform. Sometimes home problems and life events (e.g. divorce, separation, death, illness, pregnancy or marriage) will intrude and cause any person temporarily to underperform (Stein 1995).

The capacity to problem-solve and seek help becomes increasingly diffi-cult as we become overburdened. This type of stress leads to dysfunctional behaviour. The third stage of stress is when the individual is paralysed and becomes non-productive. Work or study ceases to be efficient, even though the individual may sometimes appear to have an appearance of busyness. A cynical or aggressive attitude can also develop, with the person becoming unwilling to co-operate or relate to others. The worst scenario can lead to psychosomatic illness, ulcers, backache, migraine and sometimes to heart attacks and strokes. Frequent absences, days off, alcoholism, depression and anxiety can occur. Baker (1984) terms these three kinds of stress 'optimal', 'dysfunctional' and 'paralytic'. Extreme emotional exhaustion has also been called 'burnout' and the effects of stress in the helping professions has been well researched (Ramsay and Holloway 1998). Counsellors in organizations will need to safeguard their own stress levels, particularly when dealing with very disturbed students who are being supported long-term.

Colleges of further and higher education are constantly changing – either growing rapidly, offering education to ever-increasing numbers of students, or contracting, with reductions in student numbers creating commensurate reductions in staffing with associated job losses and distress. Constant reorganization, inspections, alterations in the academic syllabus, site changes, mergers and acquisitions of new buildings can cause an organization to be seemingly very dynamic yet also very stressful. For individual members of staff, much will depend on their position in the hierarchy, as they may or may not be able to control events; other factors such as innate psychological resilience, or the quality of the support from family or home will, however, also play a role in mediating the stresses of an ever-changing environment.

This modern transformation of educational organizations into businesses, with a focus on productivity and high student throughput, can tax many staff. When this increased workload is combined with a feeling that many staff have no voice in major decisions, stress reactions may sometimes occur.

Conditions of employment have certainly changed in higher and further education establishments. Academic staff are now expected to work longer hours, teach more students and be more research-focused and financially productive in obtaining funding for projects. Administrative staff also face task overload, with vacant posts often not being filled, and frequent reorganization resulting in an ever-increasing flow of work. Greater accountability generally also adds to the stress.

Time management can be problematic for staff, given the number of unscheduled interruptions, phone calls and committee meetings which all detract from the primary tasks of teaching, research or administration. Other aspects of routine organizational life, such as negotiating with colleagues, visits from management, report and memo writing may also cause stress to particular individuals already under pressure. There often seems very little time for personal reflection and the traditional concept of a university or college being a sleepy institution where academics spent the bulk of their time delivering a few lectures, reading or writing in the library and contemplating their subject in depth is now, sadly, rapidly fading into oblivion. Dr Shirley Fisher (1994) has documented how stress in academic life affects staff and students, demonstrating the interconnectedness of life events, work efficiency and health.

Workplace counselling and staff support

Carroll emphasized the need to separate out those stress factors which are operative within a particular individual, and those which are caused directly by the work situation, such as poor management, the organization of the work itself, redundancy or downsizing, organizational change or sexual harassment (Carroll 1996).

The counselling service in a university or college also plays an important role in staff support. Most of these services include some element of staff counselling, whether this is explicit or implicit. There is little or no literature on this aspect of the counselling service and so the author will describe the types of staff cases presenting to one counselling service (Stein 1997b) where three hours a week are allocated for staff counselling. Twelve members of staff sought counselling in 1996–7 and this is shown in Table 4.1.

The table shows that seven, or just over half (58 per cent) of the staff counselled had personal problems that would probably have occurred

Table 4.1 Consultations by university staff members, 1996–7

Sex		Reason for consultation	Relevance of work issues as a cause
1	F	Bereavement (loss of parent)	Nil
2	F	Bereavement (loss of parent)	Nil
3	F	Bereavement (loss of parent)	Nil
4	F	Work stress/bereavement (loss of parent)	Work overload/work demoralization
5	F	Depression (psychiatric admission)	Nil
6	M	Depression (marital breakdown)	Nil
7	M	Alcohol problem (difficult home)	Nil
8	F	Anxiety due to extra-marital affair	Nil
9	M	Sexual harassment (perpetrator referral by his manager)	Disruption caused by client
10	M	Denial of promotion	Anger at 'system' and work overload
11	F	Work overload	Anger at management
12	F	Reluctant transfer to another site and work and childcare disruption	Anger at management

anyway, irrespective of the work context. All staff, however, reported varying degrees of underperformance in the workplace at the initial consultation.

In five cases, the reason for consultation involved problems relating to, and caused by, the work setting. One member of staff came with work stress as a presenting cause, but it soon became apparent that she also had bereavement issues that needed clinical support. Once these were dealt with, the work issues could be better handled. One client was an alleged perpetrator in a sexual harassment case, who was referred to the counselling service by his manager. He felt angry and abused by what he saw as a mis-understanding in the workplace, aggravated by university policies. The other three came with: a feeling of being constantly stressed by the workload; a feeling of being denied promotion by a manager perceived as unsympathetic; and childcare and personal difficulties following a stressful work relocation from an inner to an outer London campus. Where appro-priate, and with the client's permission, liaison took place with personnel and management. Within the counselling, stress management strategies were explored (Ellis *et al.* 1997). All felt supported by having access to a confidential staff counselling service within the working day, and a case example of one staff client is given below.

Elizabeth was a mature female academic who seemed to have lost her ability to lecture. She was suffering work stress and work overload, was underperforming, and experienced panic attacks before teaching. This was in marked contrast to an excellent employment record and high job satisfaction of many years' standing. At the time of consultation she was considering various options, including leaving her university post.

In our six counselling sessions Elizabeth discovered her need to mourn her mother, who had died six months previously. At the time of the death, the pressure of work permitted her only a week's leave to cope with her personal grief. On her return, and to escape the pain, she immersed herself entirely in her lecturing. In the initial counselling she seemed to be both traumatized and depressed, denying many feelings related to her mother and her death. Bereavement counselling was offered and this permitted Elizabeth to ventilate her tremendous feelings of guilt. She had been alerted to her mother's worsening condition but had arrived too late to see her alive. She felt guilty at not having spent more time with her, and expressed ambivalent feelings towards her sister, who had been privileged to offer nursing care to their mother. She also saw her GP who prescribed antidepressants and gave her two weeks' leave from work. It is noteworthy that she chose to continue with the counselling during her leave.

After six sessions, Elizabeth had worked through the different stages of the grieving process (Parkes 1972 and Stedeford 1991). She was able, after the fourth session, to meet with her sister and start a more honest and open relationship and to rediscover the closeness between them. She returned to her teaching and is once more an energetic and committed lecturer. She was also better equipped to handle the stress in her university department, as it was undergoing a period of restructuring.

Offering a staff counselling service within a university or college can be perceived as helpful because counsellor and client share common assumptions and knowledge of the workplace. Workplace counselling has been described as more of a triadic relationship, with client, counselling and the organization in a threeway relationship (Carroll 1996).

Further research and evaluation is needed to determine whether the percentage in this study (42 per cent of staff presenting with work problems and 58 per cent of staff presenting with personal problems) is common generally and whether it is a replicable figure. It suggests that, provided counsellors are well trained and experienced, they should be able to deal with problems among staff as, clinically, they do not differ substantially from those among the general student population. It is also likely that considerably more university and college staff members are experiencing distress concerning their work or personal lives but are either containing it or taking it elsewhere.

Conclusion

This chapter has touched upon aspects of student empowerment in counselling and the benefits of using the Egan model in brief focused work. Staff counselling support and a consideration of some specific factors causing stress in an organization have also been explored. University and college counsellors should ensure they acquire skills in dealing with stress management, bereavement, homesickness, exam anxiety and relationship difficulties which will form a considerable part of the clinical workload. The containing nature of the educational institution, with its diverse pastoral care systems, will play a vital role in supporting the work of the counsellor (O'Carroll 1997), as will good professional supervision and psychiatric consultancy. GPs and counsellors will need to collaborate closely, particularly if more serious cases of psychiatric disorder are not to be missed (Sheldon 1994). Clinical counselling within the context of an educational institution entails much more than a simple dyadic relationship between counsellor and client.

Acknowledgements

I should like to acknowledge my personal mentors: Isca Salzberger-Wittenberg, Hans Hoxter, Francesca Inskipp and Mary Banks.

Bibliography

Allen, A. (1995) *Handbook for Personal Tutors*, London: Student Services, University of Greenwich.

Baker, R. (1984) *Stress in Welfare Work*, National Childrens Home Occasional Paper No. 5.

Bell, E. (1996) *Counselling in Further and Higher Education*, Buckingham: Open University Press.

Carroll, M. (1996) *Workplace Counselling*, London: Sage Publications.

Cartwright, S. and Cooper, C. (1997) *Managing Workplace Stress*, Thousand Oaks: Sage Publications.

Clarkson, P. (1995) *The Therapeutic Relationship*, London: Whurr Publishers Ltd.

Egan, G. (1990) *The Skilled Helper*, Pacific Grove: Brooks/Cole Publishing Company.

—— (1994) *The Skilled Helper*, Pacific Grove: Brooks/Cole Publishing Company.

Ellis, A. *et al.* (1997) *Stress Counselling: A Rational Emotive Behaviour Approach*, London and Herndon, VA: Cassell.

Fisher, S. (1989) *Homesickness, Cognition and Health*, Hove: Lawrence Erlbaum Associates, Publishers.

—— (1994) *Stress in Academic Life: The Mental Assembly Line*, Bristol, PA, USA and Buckingham: The Society for Research into Higher Education and Open University Press.

Goldberg, D. and Huxley, P. (1980) *Mental Illness in the Community: The Pathway to Psychiatric Care*, London: Tavistock.

Heyno, A. (1997) 'Why do our students fear failure more than death?' *Independent*, 2 October.

Lago, C. and Thompson, J. (1996) *Race, Culture and Counselling*, Buckingham: Open University Press.

Malleson, N. (1963) 'The influence of emotional factors on achievement in university education', *Sociological Review Monograph*, No. 7, Keele: University of Keele.

O'Carroll, L. (1997) 'Psychodynamic counselling in an educational setting: containing, transference and clientele' in J. Lees (ed.), *Psychodynamic Counselling*, London: Routledge: 303–19.

Palmer, S. (1997) 'Stress counselling and management: past, present and future' in S. Palmer and V. Varma (eds), *The Future of Counselling and Psychotherapy*, London: Sage Publications: 82–111.

Parkes, M. (1972) *Bereavement Studies of Grief in Adult Life*, Harmondsworth: Penguin Books.

Quinn, R.D. (1950) *Psychotherapists' Expressions as an Index to the Quality of Early Therapeutic Relationships*, unpublished doctoral dissertation, University of Chicago.

Ramsay, R. and Holloway, F. (1998) 'Mental health services', in G. Stein and G. Wilkinson (eds), *General Adult Psychiatry Volume 2*, Royal College of Psychiatrists College Seminars Series, London: Gaskell: 1274–333.

Rickinson, B. (1997) 'Evaluating the effectiveness of counselling intervention with final year undergraduates', *Counselling Psychology Quarterly*, 10(3): 271–85.

Rogers, C. (1957) 'The necessary and sufficient conditions of therapeutic personality change', *Journal of Consulting Psychology*, 21: 95–103.

Rose, S. (1997) 'Psychological debriefing history and methods', *Counselling*, February: 48–51.

Samuels, A. (1997) 'Pluralism and the future of psychotherapy', in S. Palmer and V. Varma (eds), *The Future of Counselling and Psychotherapy*, London: Sage Publications: 132-52.

Salzberger-Wittenberg, I. (1983) *Emotional Experience of Learning and Teaching*, London: Routledge and Kegan Paul.

Seeman, J. (1954) 'Counsellor judgements of therapeutic process and outcome', in C.R. Rogers and R.F. Dymond (eds), *Psychotherapy and Personality Change*, Chicago: University of Chicago Press: Chapter 7.

Sheldon, M. (1994) 'Counselling and psychotherapy', in I. Pullen and G. Wilkinson *et al.* (eds), *Psychiatry and General Practice Today*, London: Royal College of Psychiatrists and Royal College of General Practitioners: 280–93.

Stedeford, A. (1991) 'Counselling, death and bereavement', in W. Dryden *et al.* (eds), *Handbook of Counselling in Britain*, London: Routledge.

Stein, S. (1991) 'An enquiry into the relevance of the Egan model of counselling for the Thames Polytechnic Counselling Service', unpublished MA thesis, University of Greenwich.

—— (1995) 'Coping with exam stress', *Law Journal*, University of Greenwich, 1(2), June.

—— (1997a) 'The annual report of the Counselling, Advisory and Health Service, student services', London: University of Greenwich.

—— (1997b) 'Staff counselling 1996–7', unpublished paper, University of Greenwich.

Organisation
UKCOSA: The Council for International Education
9–17 St. Albans Place
London, N1 0NX
Tel: 0171-226 3762
Fax: 0171-226 3373

5   Brief psychodynamic counselling in educational settings

Alex Coren

Introduction

It is perhaps unsurprising that in the field of therapeutic counselling in educational settings brief or focal counselling has increasingly become popular as the treatment of choice, irrespective of any time constraints imposed on the counsellor by her employment agency. Not only does it capture the developmental fluidity of students, it also parallels the student's experience of learning, a beginning, middle and end all too often being addressed simultaneously. This remains true of counsellors of whatever therapeutic orientation; for those coming from a psychodynamic perspective, however, while they may have much to contribute to both the theory and technique of focal therapies, they may also have much to unlearn.

For psychoanalysis, brief therapy is nothing less than the return of the repressed. What has been repressed is the history of the profession where short and active treatments were both popular and, in the main, successful. While psychoanalysis may be uncomfortable with the undoing of this particular repression, psychodynamic counsellors have welcomed the opportunity and challenge that this represents and are increasingly developing a body of knowledge and clinical practice which incorporates fundamental psychoanalytic concepts while at the same time adapting them to a more focused time frame. In this they are returning to the founding fathers, and mothers, of the profession.

Psychoanalysis and brief therapy

In 1906, the eminent conductor Bruno Walter, curiously at a time in his life when he was able to 'enjoy a comfortable middle class existence . . . and become a contented bourgeois . . . [enjoying] matrimonial happiness, the birth of our children [and] an economically untroubled existence', was 'attacked by an arm ailment':

Medical science called it a professional cramp, but it looked deucedly like an incipient paralysis. The rheumatic/neuralgic pain became so violent that I could no longer use my right arm for conducting or piano playing. I went from one prominent doctor to another. Each one confirmed the presence of psychogenic elements in my malady. I submitted to any number of treatments, from mudbaths to magnetism, and finally decided to call on *Professor Sigmund Freud*, resigned to submit to months of soul searching. The consultation took a course I had not foreseen. Instead of questioning me about sexual aberrations in infancy, as my layman's ignorance had led me to expect, *Freud examined my arm briefly*. I told him my story, feeling certain that he would be professionally interested in a possible connection between my actual physical affliction and a wrong I had suffered more than a year before.

Instead, he asked me if I had ever been to Sicily. When I replied that I had not he said that it was very beautiful and interesting, and more Greek than Greece itself. In short I was to leave that very evening, forget about my arm and the Opera, and do nothing for a few weeks but use my eyes. I did as I was told. Mindful of Freud's instructions [he went to Sicily] I endeavoured not to think of my affliction. I was aided by the powerful and exciting effect of my first meeting with Hellenism, which burst upon my eye and soul from every side. . . . In the end my soul and mind were greatly benefited by the additional knowledge I had gained of Hellenism, but not my arm. . . . When I got back to Vienna I poured out my troubles to Freud. His advice was to conduct –

' . . . But I can't move my arm.'
  'Try it at any rate.'
'And what if I should have to stop?'
  'You won't have to stop.'
'Can I take upon myself the responsibility of possibly upsetting a
  performance?'
'I'll take the responsibility.'

And so I did a little conducting with my right arm, then with my left, and occasionally with my head. . . . There were times when I forgot my arm over the music. I noticed that at my next session with Freud he attached particular importance to my forgetting. . . . I tried to familiarise myself with Freud's ideas and to learn from him. . . . So, by dint of much effort and confidence I finally succeeded in finding my way back to my profession.

(Walter 1947: 164–8, my italics)

In a short time Bruno Walter had overcome his neurosis. The whole treatment consisted of five to six interviews.

This, of course, was in no way atypical of a psychoanalytical consultation at that time: in 1908 Gustav Mahler's treatment consisted of one four-hour session. The early training analyses, including Freud's own self-analysis, were very brief.

As Garcia (1990) has pointed out the majority of contemporary analytical psychotherapists may well have approached Walter far differently from Freud:

> more in line with Walter's own expectations, that is, what Walter calls soul searching, or what we would call intensive dynamic therapy. Despite (or I suspect because of) being the founder of psychoanalysis, Freud was far from being an inflexible despot when it came to its therapeutic application. He happened to believe that psychoanalysis as a therapy was at best first among equals.

Garcia has termed Freud's treatment of Walter the 'neglect and counter-stimulation' technique, in many ways similar to the way in which contemporary brief therapists deal with resistance, therapeutic passivity and dependence. In this sense Freud was the original brief therapist.

How has it come about that, as psychoanalytic therapists, we are now so suspicious, uncomfortable and uneasy with the idea of brief treatment, and have come to regard it as somehow an inferior and diluted version of the real thing, often only to be used when we have no choice or because our funding agencies demand it of us?

If we look at modern-day brief therapists who advocate a great deal of activity on the part of the therapist, a confidence in technique and outcome which is conveyed to the patient, where resistances are attacked directly and material is encouraged, we can see this is very similar to the early Freud. What changed of course was the 'problem' of resistance and transference, and how to deal with it. Free association, defence analysis, the transference neurosis, ensured that therapies became longer and longer, more rigorous, and less overtly challenging or supportive. The rest, as they say, is history. Davanloo (1978) suggests that something has gone badly wrong in that, as he puts it, 'we have lost the art of curing people briefly'.

Davanloo goes on to suggest that in response to these 'problems' (e.g. Breuer's treatment of Anna O, where she developed a phantom pregnancy, believing Breuer to be the father and he retreated in alarm), therapists have become passive in technique, in accepting the increasing length of treatment, and 'in their ability to explain, not merely to a lay audience but also to themselves what happens in the analytic process'. Seen from one perspective, therapeutic passivity, regression, free association, required longer to analyse. Equally, if it was longer it had to be more rigorous; what other rationale could there be for it? It would appear that the more we learn, or know, about psychoanalysis, the more we have come to accept a certain inevitability that therapies will become longer, when in fact we could infer that our increasing knowledge should make them shorter.

This development, coming when it did, accompanied grandiose claims as to the efficacy and necessity of psychoanalysis. In the field of education the recommendation was made that all teachers be psychoanalysed before being allowed into the classroom. But as Davanloo suggests, therapeutic passivity was not the only choice available: therapy could have become more active, and briefer. There is a long and honourable tradition of brief psychoanalytic psychotherapy which tries to counteract passivity in technique by becoming active, but this met, and still meets, with a great deal of resistance. It is unfortunate that much of the literature on brief psychoanalytic psychotherapy still appears to believe that the aim and purpose of short-term work is to convince the patient of the necessity for longer-term therapy. One of the difficulties of viewing brief therapy in this historical context is that it becomes merely a footnote or a lesser branch of applied psychoanalysis, rather than something different: separate but of equal value. Despite this, it is interesting to note the current rediscovery, and interest in, the early brief analysts such as Sandor Ferenczi.

Student counselling and brief therapy

In student counselling nationally, the average number of sessions is between four and six. This clearly makes the work of counselling in educational settings somewhat different in form from much of psycho-dynamic brief therapy, where anything from a dozen to forty or fifty sessions is the rule. It may well be that a distinction needs to be drawn between a brief consultation which may take four sessions, and brief planned focal therapy which can take considerably longer, although both have pre-set time limits. If we look at the literature on selection criteria for brief therapy, theorists divide into two camps, the conservative and the radical. These differ essentially on the issue of pathology, conservatives believing that brief therapy can help, but only in limited situations, while the radical position is that brief therapy is able to benefit a wide range of problems and patients. At its most extreme, the radical camp appears to share the hubris of the early psychoanalysts, that brief therapy can cure everything.

In general, brief therapy looks towards a set of conditions:

- a circumscribed problem;

- motivation;
- psychological mindedness;
- intelligence;
- a capacity to establish relationships;
- flexibility of defences;
- an Oedipal focus;
- a capacity to form a treatment alliance;
- a capacity to reflect;
- some recognition that problems have an emotional content;
- a certain introspection (if not curiosity) about oneself;
- a capacity to tolerate frustration or anxiety.

Amongst the conservative group contraindications may include:

- severe pre-genital problems;
- exclusively borderline pathology (involving extreme difficulties around the frustration of time limits);
- difficulties with termination because of deep-seated or complex problems regarding loss;
- exclusive reliance on projection;
- massive denial;
- a major reliance on acting out in dealing with psychological conflicts.

What we are left with is a patient who is relatively healthy, well-functioning, with a well-defined and circumscribed area of difficulty, who is intelligent, psychologically minded and well motivated for change. Essentially, therapists are all looking for the same patient, who is proving to be eternally elusive. These criteria would gladden the heart of any therapist, long- or short-term . . . if only patients would play their part.

Counsellors in educational settings must inevitably be drawn to the radical position. This is partly because, as I will describe, brief therapy can transcend all but the most severe pathology. However, another reason is that in the field of student counselling, counsellors have no choice but to be in the radical camp. The high level of demand, together with the fact that counselling in educational settings is generally open access and needs to take into account the educational calendar, ensures that brief therapy is the treatment of necessity. Additionally, the majority of students only want (as opposed to what their therapists think they need) brief counselling. Having said that, it needs to be noted that David Malan, of the radical brief therapy camp, advocates a guideline of twenty sessions for 'an ordinary [straightforward] patient with an experienced therapist', and thirty sessions for 'an ordinary patient with an inexperienced therapist' (Malan 1982b:

108). Psychodynamic counsellors can take heart from Winnicott, who talks about strict time limits without recourse to diagnostic categories, and about the importance of surprise, play, process and metaphor in these brief consultations. Infuriatingly, however, Winnicott, as always, doesn't tell us how to do it.

Many counselling services in educational settings have no 'filter' and offer open access to all students, and frequently staff, of the institution. Generally there is no choice regarding eligibility, or exclusion, on the basis of pathology or problem, and goals may appear, and have to be, necessarily modest – although not, I believe, insubstantial or superficial. Working in this context and setting, the absence of eligibility criteria based on pathology or symptom may well be advantageous. Rigorous selection may well have excluded Jeffrey.

Jeffrey, a 20-year-old second-year physicist, was referred by his GP who described him as significantly depressed and becoming increasingly socially withdrawn: staying in his room, not eating and from time to time engaged in minor acts of self-harm (cutting his arm with a blunt knife). He was arousing a great deal of anxiety and his GP wanted him to be seen as soon as possible; this was in contrast with Jeffrey himself, who clearly didn't want to be seen at all, urgently or not.

I was confronted by a pale, gaunt, ascetic young man, who clearly did not want to be either at Oxford or in my consulting room. He was passive, morose, and significantly uncommunicative in the initial consultation.

I saw him for a total of three sessions over a five-week period and the story which we laboriously pieced together ran as follows. Born in the North of England, he moved frequently in his first few years, his father being a systems analyst in a computer firm, before eventually settling in a small town in the North of England. He lived, seemingly uneventfully, with his parents and younger sister, until his father died suddenly when Jeffrey was aged 14. Jeffrey threw himself into his academic work, watched over by a mother who became increasingly 'pushy'. He didn't want to be at university and suspected nefarious forces were conspiring to push him here: his mother, and his school, which he thought had an informal link with his college. While academically successful in his first year, he consciously avoided making new friendships or taking part in the many activities which the university had to offer. Interestingly, what was very striking in his description of his current life was that he would have nothing to do with anything associated with the university, but would occasionally attend social events in town (rather than gown), which appeared to give him the comfortable, yet not wholly pleasant, experience of maintaining an identification with home.

He was angry and dismissive of the 'ritual, pomp and stuffiness' of university life and wanted nothing to do with it. He continued with a desultory relationship with a girlfriend at home, who appeared to provide only comfort and relief from his sufferings, rather than any substantial pleasure. It also, of course, gave him reason not to engage in any social activities in college. He was becoming uninterested in work, but felt trapped. He was almost compelled to be here but didn't want to be – and it was of interest that when this was said I was unclear whether he was referring to university or the consulting room. It will come as no surprise to learn that he was also passive and reluctant to engage in the process of therapy, other than to present himself to me.

When I commented on this, Jeffrey mentioned being temperamentally shy and self-effacing, 'a bit like my father'. His father had attended a provincial university and hated it. Eventually, Jeffrey thought his father had worked himself to death doing something he didn't enjoy. It was as though Jeffrey was at university for his father, not only because he was doing something without enjoyment, but also because, while it was his mother who was experienced as being the 'pushy' parent, he believed his father would have been quietly proud of him. But in order to maintain an identification with him, Jeffrey took great pains to both dislike the place, and avoid engaging in anything associated with it, which might indeed be fatal. For by engaging with it he ran the risk of betraying his father's memory. His impotent anger and resentment, turned primarily against the self, was something he couldn't let go of; it was a perverse way of keeping his father alive in a moribund state. His dead father accompanied him everywhere. He knew his father didn't like physics either, and would, had he lived, have felt exactly the same as Jeffrey.

Jeffrey couldn't let go of his resentment because it combined an attack on himself via his detachment (an unconscious equation of working hard and 'being in the world' = killing people), resentment of others (who had live fathers, or resenting mothers who hadn't been able to keep fathers alive), as well as maintaining an identification with a father in fantasy who hated university, would have been proud of him, but who was dead. Living would mean psychologically burying his father and coming to terms with the loss. By the end of our third session Jeffrey was doing just that: playing in a college band, in the college football team and occasionally doing some physics.

What happened? Was this a transference cure or a flight into health? I think neither. I was very active with him: I wasn't going to be the dead father whom Jeffrey attempted to keep alive via paralysis in our sessions. I told him we had a limited number of sessions; he was forced to choose both if and how to use them, and their frequency (this transference to how little or much is available and how the student perceives and uses it is a very important and helpful therapeutic tool). The initial frustration and anger to the limited work (understandably somewhat muted in Jeffrey's case) set the tone. In part through my activity, Jeffrey was angry that I had disturbed his melancholy reverie, and that I was modelling or implying an alternative way of identifying with his father which involved being alive (or active). I attempted to link the mute anger/passivity and frustration with anxiety (i.e. what was the nature of the anxiety being defended against?). What would happen if Jeffrey lived? Would father or father's memory die? Was the only possible link and source of identification with his father a foreclosure of his own development?

He was annoyed with me for not colluding with this in our sessions. I wasn't going to have dead sessions. What was central was this issue of passivity/anger and its expression in three linked areas: first, the process of sessions: the here and now/what was going on, or not, between us; second, his developmental history (his family, his background, his dead father and what attachment to university/another place might represent); and third, his current functioning (his conscious effort to have no part in university life or to socialize). Since his father's death, he wanted to maintain an illusion of stasis and paralysis in all these areas, not least his therapy. Metaphorically, in sessions, we were continuously addressing these three themes at once. For instance, when we talked about the process between him and me, I was aware that we were also addressing the other two sides of this triangle: his past history and his current life outside the consulting room.

The issue of loss in relation to Jeffrey is an interesting theoretical point in relation to brief counselling. Losing me, as something to be worked through, didn't exist, partly because he never really had me. The setting, being active, pointing out what he was attempting to do with the process and how that may link with his past and present life, addressed issues of loss and possible meanings of his deadness.

This is not an atypical consultation in student counselling. Why does it seem to work, given the limited goals and time? Partly because it is appropriate for the context in which counsellors in educational settings work, but also because it speaks to the adolescent/young adult's developmental drive. Many young adults, having just left home and their families, do not necessarily wish, or need, to be pulled back into what can be experienced as a regressively frightening (or comforting – which can be equally problematic at this age) relationship. At a time in their lives when they need to go out and face and actively master the world, the risk exists of encouraging them to enter into a long-term regressive therapeutic relationship which might be experienced by the young person as a tyrannical demand that can only be met by a defeated or hostile compliance. However difficult it is for therapists to accept, real life happens outside the consulting room.

Issues for psychodynamic counsellors practising brief therapy

The issue of context is an important one, and brings up the subject of transference. It is useful and important to distinguish between transference as ubiquitous (that is, it's everywhere) and the transference neurosis, which is a specific illusion of the therapeutic setting. Therapists, despite their occasional protestations, can actually be quite active in either encouraging or discouraging this. In these brief consultations, I do not encourage a transference neurosis; what needs to be worked with, as with Jeffrey, is the transference to education, to one's own development, joining and leaving an institution, the institution itself and what the counsellor might represent in it, and to the setting. If transference is ubiquitous then one can have both a transference and counter-transference to brief therapy. This then becomes the process of therapeutic encounters in education; not who I am (or what the client neurotically invests in me or turns me into), but what the setting, or I in that setting, may stand for. Transference to the setting is what becomes important; feelings about receiving help, limited help, not being encouraged to regress, issues about ending that are in evidence from the beginning, become the predominant themes for the therapy. In academic settings one is particularly fortunate in this area, as education is about developmental fluidity: in education you cannot 'stand still' so the setting actually facilitates active brief interventions.

These brief consultations are the most productive use of the adolescent/ young adult's developmental drive. According to Erikson (1981), one of the major paradigms at this stage in life is intimacy or isolation (that is, working out where you are on that continuum). Thus the young person's wish not to make too great a commitment (having just left their families, and we mustn't forget that going to university remains one of the most acceptable reasons for leaving home), rather than being seen as a problem, becomes not merely much more understandable, but a potential solution, and can be fostered by a non-regressive partnership in brief work. In this sense it would be important for the therapist to recognize the need to take herself out of the limelight, however difficult that may be at times, and to assume a more oblique, third-party role. Students, and young adults generally, may need a haven away from the intimacy of the family which they have frequently just left, as well as from the intensity of the tutorial or teaching relationship, which can be experienced as particularly intrusive.

Working in this way has major implications for therapeutic technique. Of central importance is the early discovery and mutual agreement of a central therapeutic focus. Moreover, this needs to be a central focus with which all material can be either linked or associated. This is necessarily frustrating for the therapist who has been trained in longer-term work, as it means jettisoning all material not directly associated with the focus. The focus must encompass the 'Triangle of Insight', that is, the current life situation, linking with the past history and with what is happening in the room, the active present if you like. This triangle links with another psychodynamic triangle: the impulse, the defence against it and consequent anxiety. This becomes the focus of the work. Some brief therapists would say that if the focus cannot be determined, or if it is vague or diffuse, then brief therapy is contraindicated, but since diffuse vagueness is a condition of adolescence it merely becomes part of the therapeutic process.

Therapeutic activity maintains the focus, prevents regression and helps to keep the emotional tension high. As Davanloo (1978) has said: 'we can't wait for the material to bubble up'. Regression and dependence are minimized by sitting facing each other, the spacing of appointments, with, as often as not, the client choosing how regularly to meet (and the psychological significance of the outcome of that decision discussed), and knowledge that the treatment is finite, which deals with the ambiguity over the ending of the treatment and any anxiety around it.

It is important to believe, and in some way communicate to the client, that a great deal can be achieved in such a short space of time. Counselling in educational settings must guard against the merely cerebral: counselling must never replicate a tutorial. It must make, or attempt to make, substantial emotional contact with the client, otherwise it becomes yet another intellectual exercise and is approached and dealt with by the client in the same way. The feelings towards the process have to be central; they may well be characteristic ways of relating to people in one's current life; they demonstrate how they have related to other people in the past, and how dysfunctional and inappropriate these ways of relating may be. Consequently, early manifestations of the transference (especially to the setting and process as opposed to the neurotic transference) have to be interpreted and one has to speak to the client's conscious ego (often to prevent the development of an incipient transference neurosis and to put the client on guard against dependency and regression) as well as metaphorically to the unconscious.

A further potentially problematic area, if you have been trained in longer-term work, is the concept of working through. Clearly in brief work there is little of this process, which is thought to be central to longer-term therapy. In brief therapy the working through is more likely to begin after the therapy is finished, but this may be little different from longer-term therapy: working through begins after the last session. In this sense brief therapy mimics life which can be seen as an extending period of working through: we get on with the process of continually having to metabolize our emotional experiences. However, since educational settings allow for developmental pro- and regression during the person's membership of the institution, as developmental obstacles are addressed, it may be advisable to view the therapeutic model as one of 'topping up' rather than a working-through – i.e. a short burst of intensive work with the option of coming back for topping up at some later date. This also aids the client's transference to the setting: they can hold the counsellor as a potential sanctuary, if they so wish, throughout their academic careers. However, given how few students in my experience seek 'topping up', it may well be that 'topping up' is more about the counsellor reassuring themselves than being helpful for the client.

One of the aims of brief counselling is to enable the client to internalize the experience, and for a different version of themselves to emerge. However, doing so can be risky both for the therapist and for the client. The client risks being surprised about themselves. For many clients in educational settings, learning something new about themselves is potentially rather exciting. Brief counselling in education then becomes about the discovery of alternative scripts as well as normalizing emotional experience.

David Malan (1992) has suggested that for Oedipal patients separation and dependence are less likely to be issues, whereas with pre-Oedipal ones loss and separation are constant factors but that both are amenable to brief treatments. Counsellors need to think of the context and the goals of any individual treatment and to remind themselves that in brief therapy they are not engaged in character analysis or open-ended psychotherapy. However, the approach can transcend pathology as in the case of Julie.

Julie, a 36-year-old graduate student, within a chapter of finishing her thesis, presented with depression and an inability to write, which after four years on her thesis had become a major problem. Briefly (and when writing this I found the brevity a problem because I had to leave out a lot of what I considered to be the interesting bits; not unlike the frustration of brief therapy) she was the eldest child of a humble West Country family. Her father died when Julie was 13, and she and her younger brother were then brought up by her midwife mother who never remarried. She did well at school and was an academically successful undergraduate, despite disliking the university and becoming severely depressed in her final year, leading to in-patient and subsequently day-patient hospitalization. During her twenties she had been a teacher and worked in publishing, but suffered a further depressive episode just after she became engaged to be married. She required further psychiatric treatment and the marriage was called off. Subsequently, in her early thirties, she had three years of counselling, which had clearly been helpful, 'but . . . '. She struck me as having been an unconsciously depressed woman for some considerable time, leading me to wonder whether depression can be characterological rather than necessarily related to loss.

I offered her four sessions, which immediately provoked barely concealed frustration. Within a short space of time we were into the issue of whether, had she been more interesting, lively and engaging, I would have offered her more. Would her father still be alive had she been able to be more interesting, lively or engaging? His loss was still a source of great distress and bemusement to her. This was a constant theme in our work, but only peripherally linked to what became the central focus. In my initial consultation with her, she had mentioned, 'Time is running out', and 'feeling physically sick' in relation to her thesis, which, together with other linked material, led me to suggest to her that her thesis was the baby she never had, which made her reluctance to relinquish it understandable. Over the last 4–5 years she had so tenderly nurtured it; no wonder she didn't want to let go of it. This was a phantom thesis baby as opposed to the real baby she in reality wished for. Relinquishing this baby would be like killing it off.

We can see how this therapeutic focus spoke to many aspects of this woman's life: issues of creativity and procreativity, ambivalent competition with her own mother over babies and careers (mother was not at all academic), and the pervasive issue of loss, including the risk that she would run in any potential successful relationship which might produce a real baby. This latter carried with it the danger of having to replace her fantasized and foreclosed relationship with her father. Her history, her presenting problem (work) and her current life and relationships (which by her own account she called 'sterile and barren'), and her relationship with me, were able to be addressed in this limited focus and time. What sort of baby could we produce in four sessions? Would it be good enough and vital enough to continue living beyond our limited time together? Would she have to, and could she, relinquish it at the end of our time?

I had to continue to work with Julie's frustration towards me regarding not only the limited time and what that represented, but also the limited self which she was able to present to me, which we both recognized as necessary in preventing a form of attachment developing. At one point she mused about the loss of her father, and her capacity to be infatuated by men, to which I said, 'And we don't want that to happen here given the limited time available', to which she replied, 'No, I can't allow that to happen.' The 'I' in that sentence referred, I think, to us both (speaking to our conscious egos).

A few weeks after finishing with Julie, I read in the university gazette that she had completed her thesis. Clearly my goals were modest. The inability to complete her thesis was what she brought, but I hope in addressing that, we were also addressing fundamental conflicts and dilemmas in her life.

Conclusion

Counselling in university settings gives people a taste of seeing, thinking and feeling about themselves in new ways, all within metaphors of education and development.

Much can be achieved in these brief, surprising, psychodynamically informed interventions, but they should not be viewed as generic solutions. The danger exists, particularly if brief counselling is seen merely as an aid to solve the problem of crowded waiting rooms and long waiting lists, of fitting the client into a therapeutic modality, rather than the other way round. It also runs the risk of reinforcing the belief that it is not the best that we can offer and is less than the patient needs. The emphasis then becomes more on technique than exploration or reflection. Unfortunately, some of the literature on brief focal therapies, more particularly the technical onslaught against therapeutic resistance employed by some schools, has the flavour of indoctrination rather than play, and we know indoctrination leads to compliance. Clients can incorporate their therapists in a manner analogous to pets resembling their owners. There is also a danger of therapeutic sadism in some of these approaches.

Another danger is that, as Terry Kupers (1981) says in 'Public Therapy', open-ended talking therapy is available to those who can afford it, while those who can't are either hospitalized, medicated or offered a form of 'brief therapy' which is viewed by practitioner and patient alike as expedient and second-best. We are currently in that position in Britain, with long waiting lists for any sort of public sector reflective emotional help. This brings with it the issue of whether therapy is about adaptation or change. (This applies to long-term therapy too, but is more concentrated in shorter term therapies.) This is an important dilemma in counselling in educational settings: is our task to return students to the academic treadmill as soon as possible (without questioning the wider institution's complicity in provoking, or at least reinforcing, the symptom), or is it to allow, and protect, some space for personal and developmental issues to be addressed? This is an extremely delicate balance, and I believe brief psychoanalytically-informed therapy can address both. For some students, of course, this is not possible, and a constant dilemma is how to manage the small minority of clients who need something else.

An ongoing debate in educational settings is the issue of who sets the framework or boundaries for, amongst other things, the length of treatment – the institution or the therapist? While Freud said that the definition of mental health was 'to love and to work', student counsellors need to consider inverting that maxim. To work and to love may be equally important. The importance of the student being able to function academically needs to be recognized, not merely from the institution's point of view, but also from the student's, for whom academic work may be a major source of both pleasure and self-esteem. The potentially problematic area is at what point do counsellors say enough is enough, and at what point do the client's emotional and developmental needs take precedence over institutional or academic ones?

Psychodynamic brief therapy/counselling is not an easy option, and involves a great deal of unlearning. Little in the longer-term psycho-dynamic counselling trainings prepares counsellors for this work, other than to view it as a diluted version of the real thing, only to be thought about when the possibility of longer-term work is not an option. Viewing the goal of brief therapy as 'helping the patient realize their need for longer-term work' is a particularly unfortunate version of this. It also comes dangerously close to indoctrination. It carries with it the danger of ignoring, or denying, the very real differences between brief psychodynami-cally informed therapy and psychoanalytic psychotherapy. These brief consultations are not about depth (although the ripples that can be caused by therapeutic surprise should not be underestimated) or about the nature and length of any existing disturbance. Given the partial focus, the more disturbed client can potentially make more use of it than longer-term therapies, where issues of loss of control, and facing one's own psychotic anxieties, can be quite frightening and lead to decompensation.

There are other reasons why brief therapy can be attractive for those who, for cultural or social reasons, are suspicious of longer-term psychotherapy:

- it conveys, amongst other things, therapeutic hope;
- it does not pathologize;
- it does not procrastinate (in the sense of recognizing that life needs to be experienced, not lived, in the consulting room).

The problem for the counsellor is how to risk being active without impingement or seduction? One of the main dangers for the counsellor in brief work is that the anxiety about being active can lead her to not being active enough and to lose the focus. Can she risk paying what feels like selective attention, and neglect seemingly meaningful material? This requires resilience, and a willingness to take charge of the therapeutic setting.

Not least of the difficulties is the seemingly promiscuous nature of the work: seeing so many people in such a short space of time imposes its own discipline and demands. Counsellors may need to be able to, if not transcend their trainings, then at least consider the possibility of entertaining alternative ways of thinking about problems and ways of working. If a client says, 'Can I be helped in such a short space of time?' (Flegenheimer 1982) and the counsellor, for whatever reason, shares this ambivalence, then the prognosis will be bleak. Brief therapy cannot merely be a concentrated version of longer-term therapies. In other words brief therapy has to be the treatment of choice, which in many settings and with particular client groups it is, and we have to be flexible in thinking about some of our uncritically accepted beliefs: if brief therapy is to be the treatment of choice it then has to be a choice of treatments. Conversely, as noted above, overzealousness in espousing the cause of brief therapies can lead to the same kind of hubris as the psychoanalysts of fifty or sixty years ago claimed in relation to analysis.

For adolescents and young adults, particularly in education, brief consultations allow the young person to proceed with age-appropriate tasks, while longer-term therapy (unless specifically indicated, needed or wanted by the young person) carries with it the danger of stultifying the maturational process (Flegenheimer 1982). The psychodynamic core of these consultations consist of a knowledge of:

- developmental theory (what stage people are at in their lives);

- transference (and its varied manifestations);
- a belief in the unconscious and the use of metaphor and symbol as powerful modes of thinking and communication;
- a belief in repetition which needs to be grasped rather than continually re-experienced;
- the central themes or leitmotifs which recur in a person's discourse;
- the use of the relationship as the paradigm for the central conflict and its potential link with the presenting problem; and, in deference to the early Freud,
- the subversive nature of surprise for both client and counsellor.

This echoes Freud's comment to Walter that sometimes we need to be able to see, not merely feel.

When Freud talked about alloying the 'pure gold' of psychoanalysis with copper in order to meet the anticipated large-scale demand, the copper he was referring to was not brief psychodynamic therapy, with its emphasis on focus and time limits, but suggestion and hypnosis. Psychodynamically oriented brief therapists frequently find it problematic to shake off this implied historical paradigm: psychoanalysis as pure = large-scale demand = dilution of purity because of expedience = brief therapies. The danger remains that brief counselling becomes viewed as somehow second-rate. Part of the problem is that, at some level, consciously or unconsciously, counsellors are encouraged to do so by the history of their profession. They are invited to see long-term therapy as rigorous, intensive and thorough, while short-term work is viewed as insubstantial and superficial, rather than to accept that these are two different modalities, no doubt with some similarities, but essentially different. Not better or worse, just different. Counsellors enshrine, if not encourage, the notion of difference in their work with patients, but they often appear to dismiss or devalue this notion between themselves.

Counsellors in educational settings have the opportunity to work creatively within a brief framework which is both normative and the treatment of choice for the majority of their clients, thus placing themselves at the frontier of developments in this emerging therapeutic field. In the final analysis, whether we are engaged in long- or short-term psychotherapy, what matters is, as Nina Coltart (1992) has said, 'trust in the process, in our technique, in our patients' . . . and, by definition, in ourselves.

Bibliography

Coltart, N. (1992) *Slouching Towards Bethlehem . . . and further psychoanalytic explorations*, London: Free Association Books.

Davanloo, H. (ed.) (1978) *Basic Principles and Techniques in Short Term Dynamic Psychotherapy*, New York: S.P. Medical and Scientific Books.

Erikson, E. (1981) *Childhood and Society*, London: Granada Press.

Flegenheimer, W.V. (1982) *Techniques of Brief Psychotherapy*, New York: Aronson.

Garcia, E.E. (1990) 'Somatic interpretation in a transference cure: Freud's treatment of Bruno Walter', *International Review of Psychoanalysis*, 17: 83–8.

Kupers, T. (1981) *Public Therapy: the practice of psychotherapy in the public mental health clinic*, New York: Free Press.

Malan, D. (1982a) *Individual Psychotherapy and the Science of Psychodynamics*, London: Butterworth.

—— (1992) *Psychodynamics, Teaching and Outcome in Brief Psychotherapy*, London: Butterworth/Heinemann.

Walter, B. (1947) *Theme and Variations*, London: Hamish Hamilton: 181–4.

6 Focusing the work

A cognitive-behavioural approach

Peter Ross

Introduction

This chapter discusses the application of Cognitive-Behavioural Therapy (CBT) to short-term clinical counselling. Many researchers (e.g. Parry 1996) assert that in numerous areas of application the evidence for CBT provides it with a significant advantage over other approaches, and commend CBT to purchasers. The commendation is particularly focused on problems which present frequently in the context of a further and higher education counselling service – depression, anxiety and bulimia nervosa (but not anorexia nervosa, where the evidence for psychodynamic therapy is better). In coming to this conclusion Parry depends heavily on Roth and Fonagy (1996). However, in the field of further and higher education the predominant counselling approach is psychodynamic, which to date has been little researched; and of course lack of evidence for other models does not imply ineffectiveness. Furthermore, methodological problems in research studies make it difficult to generalize from these findings.

CBT is not necessarily a brief therapy, but is used as such most of the time, particularly within further and higher education. The rationale for this is based on research suggesting that client ratings almost always suggest the greatest improvements being experienced from the initial six to ten sessions (summarized in Koss and Shiang 1994). In addition, evidence from the meta-research literature (summarized by Howard *et al.* 1986), is that the greatest improvements are achieved early in therapy.

The background to CBT

In terms of philosophical underpinning, CBT contains elements of the Graeco-Roman philosophy of Stoicism. The enduring Stoic insight, crucial to CBT, is that people are not emotionally disturbed so much by events, as by their beliefs about them.

Some key figures in the history of CBT are J.D. Watson, Pavlov, B.F. Skinner and Joseph Wolpe. For example, Wolpe (1982), working in the early 1950s, discovered that the simultaneous occurrence of anxiety-provoking events and a response antagonistic to anxiety, would reduce the anxiety. He applied this to phobias. His therapy, Systematic Desensitization, became both popular and effective. The patient was taught relaxation, then progressed either in real life or imagination through a gradient of feared situations which were arranged in a hierarchy of ascending difficulty.

More recent pioneers include Bandura (1982), Meichenbaum (1975), Beck *et al.* (1979, 1990) and Ellis (1962). These latter theorists have tended to integrate cognitive and behavioural approaches. Furthermore different cognitive-behavioural approaches have emerged from the research to address different disorders. Assessment is therefore crucial in deciding whether CBT is suitable and if so what form this should take. There are good overviews of CBT theory (Scott and Dryden 1996) and practice (Hawton *et al.* 1989; Lindsay and Powell 1994).

The context of further and higher education

Nowadays universities and colleges can differ markedly. Many still have their main intake from school leavers who are already in a period of late adolescent identity formation. Other institutions can have 40 per cent of their intake from 'mature' students (over 21 at entry) and 20 per cent from mature postgraduate international students. Whatever the intake the students are in the midst of development and transition, deliberately exposed to a rich mixture of competing ideas and cultures. They are under constant demand to perform new tasks using only just learned skills and to do so to tight deadlines. They are removed from long-established school, family and social relationships, and need to make new friends quickly. They may have to spend years working almost alone to gain a Ph.D. or may be required to work in changing small groups not of their choosing to gain an undergraduate degree. Moreover, these relationships are fractured by the three-term structure of most institutions.

CBT in educational settings therefore differs from CBT practised in psychiatric or psychological settings in a number of ways:

- In the clinic one can often assume a background of ongoing relationships which provide emotional support. Given the context of fractured and tentative relationships sketched above, CBT in educational settings has to put emphasis on providing an emotionally supportive relationship as well as a good working one.
- Given the diverse catchment population in educational settings, CBT

practitioners need to vary their style of joining with clients rather more than in the clinical setting.

- CBT practitioners in clinical settings normally see patients who have been assessed by a GP. In an educational setting the counsellor will often be the first person with whom the client has discussed the problem. Students are often troubled without being able to identify the nature of the problem. More time often needs to be spent on exploring 'meaning' to make explicit the nature of the problem.
- Students have to have high levels of concentration to meet regular deadlines. Concentration is often the first thing to go when anxiety and depression strike. This may not be such an issue in the established routines of the jobs of those who attend the clinic. The strategy in educational settings is to provide symptomatic relief as a priority.
- In the setting of a clinic one can usually assume ongoing attendance as required. In educational settings, terms end; while examinations, field trips and placements can also disrupt normal counselling. In educational settings therefore one must give extra emphasis to the initial assessment and in particular the client's understanding of it and its implications for the ongoing work. The client is then more able to practise informed self-help when the counsellor may not be available, or available only on the telephone. One can also set up the work in explicit modules. This way disruption matters less.

'Self-talk': a conceptual bridge between CBT and psychodynamic theory

What people say to themselves about themselves ('self-talk' in CBT) is the focus of much attention in CBT practice. Counsellors more familiar with psychodynamic concepts may find helpful some indication of how a conceptual bridge has been made between the approaches, notably by John Bowlby, whose attachment theory combined the empiricism of ethology with the subjective insights of psychoanalysis.

Mary Main (1995) has developed a semi-structured assessment interview, the Adult Attachment Interview (AAI), based on Bowlby's work on attachment and loss. The scoring depends primarily on narrative style (how people talk about and think about themselves) rather than content. Holmes (1997) suggests that attachment experience becomes internalized as 'self-narrative' and that narrative styles form the basis for the way we tell our life story as we describe ourselves and our problems to others. It has been shown that infant attachment patterns are predictive of AAI scores later in adolescence (Benoit and Parker 1994), and that such patterns transmit across generations (Fonagy *et al.* 1994). This natural assimilation is extended in counselling and forms a self-analytic or constructive self-talk function at the end of counselling (Kohut, 1984).

Assessment in CBT

As previously mentioned, assessment is important in further and higher education. From a CBT point of view assessment has the following elements when applied in this setting:

- CBT is a package of different therapies. They have much in common, but each is a CBT in its own right. The initial assessment is followed by a reassessment after each session, since, although particular techniques will often suit particular problems, it is far from being the case that they will always do so, and treatment may have to be varied.
- The CBT relationship is a teaching one. But especially for initial assessment with students, an explicit non-judgemental attitude is essential. Increasingly detailed questions draw the client's attention to what is important and from the beginning educate the client into the model.
- One will screen out clients who are so imbued with a very different way of looking at themselves that it will be less time-consuming for a counsellor and less unsettling for an already anxious client, to rule out CBT. A student who has spent months taking a psychoanalytic approach to, say, a sociology thesis and then comes for counselling might fall into this category. Why spend huge amounts of time trying to make alternative models plausible when a model has already been assimilated? The typical psychology, medical, philosophy or archaeology student already familiar with CBT concepts provides the opposite example.
- The client's ability to be able to identify and disclose thoughts, and then make a link between them and emotions is crucial to the success of CBT. So the counsellor will often be focusing on just that:

Counsellor: So, as you began to get anxious as you approached the student residence where you had the panic attack, what was going through your mind?

Client: Oh, you know, just seeing everyone looking at me. I mean, I know they don't. But that's what it feels like.

Counsellor: So, you were telling yourself everyone would be looking at you?

Client: I suppose.

Counsellor: And clearly if they were, you weren't too keen on that idea, otherwise you wouldn't have been anxious?

Client:	Right.
Counsellor:	So if we put that together: everybody will be looking at me and if they do then that will not be nice? That will be awful?
Client:	Right. It would be terrible. It is.
Counsellor:	Terrible because . . . ?
Client:	I don't know. I really don't know.
Counsellor:	Supposing you had the power to guarantee they would really think whatever you ideally wanted them to think, what would that be?
Client:	That I was great, that they liked me.
Counsellor:	No anxiety then?
Client:	No.
Counsellor:	So, let's try this for size. You approach the residence and you're thinking to yourself, 'They'll all be looking at me and they must all, all the time, like me otherwise it'll be just awful and I just couldn't stand it !'?
Client:	Yes, that's just about it.

It does not take long to unpack 'like'. For this client it means 'approve of'. These are called negative automatic thoughts. Clients often need considerable help to identify them and link them to emotions.

- Assessment has to take in the history of the problem. This is partly to check client perception of origin, even if maintenance turns out to be now more important, but also because many chronic problems are characterological and should be screened out. Short-term CBT is often best with problems of recent onset.

In summary, in an assessment one tries (1) to screen out those unsuitable for CBT; (2) to understand the problems presented, select a target problem and agree a formulation; (3) educate the client in the CBT model; (4) begin the process of change, prescribing homework as early as the end of the initial assessment. Formal questionnaires and self-report measures, though very helpful, are seldom either essential or well-tolerated by student clients. Scott and Dryden (1996) have helpful comments on self-report measures as well as other aspects of CBT assessment.

Automatic thoughts

The most simple rationale for the cognitive-behavioural model is that a person's emotional responses to aversive situations are largely determined by the view taken of them. The trigger may be external (having to face an examination) or internal ('I'm no good and never will be'). The views may be simple negative thoughts, or integrated attitudes or fundamental assumptions. Of special interest are automatic thoughts, that is to say, ones experienced as involuntary or ones so fleeting that they are barely recognized but still produce an emotional impact. Automatic thoughts can be verbal or visual, occur repeatedly and seem so utterly plausible they produce high levels of emotion. People can become hypervigilant, scanning their environment for cues to confirm their beliefs, but the low anxiety thresholds and split attention wreak havoc with academic concentration.

All types of CBT use monitoring forms to help the client develop awareness of self-talk, how it is triggered and how it produces emotion and other physiological and behavioural consequences. The A (activating event) B (beliefs) C (emotional consequences) model of Ellis (1962) is perhaps best known. Beck and Emery (1985) encourage clients to keep daily records of automatic thoughts using similar forms to recover awareness of fleeting instances through 'instant replay'. A Ph.D. student seen by the author provides an illustration. She was unable to attend university due to numerous fears. One was of travelling on the London Underground. This is her work sheet:

Situation: Approaching the train, or even sitting at home thinking of travelling.

Automatic thoughts: The train will stop between stations and I couldn't get off fast. If it even slowed down I would get so terrified I would throw up. That would be terrible. Then I'd be kept in a hospital as crazy.

Consequence: Avoiding journey and so avoiding terror.

What is the evidence?: I've never actually been sick. But I saw somebody else do it. I do get dizzy and get pins and needles and know that's the start of it.

Alternative view: Learn about hyperventilation, and how to control it.

Attributions: Making mountains out of molehills (cognitive distortion). Thinking like this, there would be something wrong with me if I didn't get anxious.

Decatastrophizing (new self-talk): If I do throw up, so what? If other people don't like it, that's their problem. Everybody throws up sometimes. They're probably far more interested in reading their newspaper than in me anyway. I can just say 'Sorry, but I'm fine' then nobody will worry. Anyway it's unlikely to happen if I practise relaxation.

This client recovered through a combination of (1) frequently repeating the restructured de-catastrophized self-talk; (2) imagining herself doing so in graded exposure situations including being on a train; (3) practising relaxation while in the real situation.

Cognitive distortions

Apart from misattributions, as illustrated above, a long list of common information processing errors (cognitive distortions) has been identified by Beck, Ellis and others. Some of these are:

Awfulizing: 'If I threw up that would be so terrible and so embarrassing I would die.'

Minimizing: 'So what if I've got a Ph.D? They probably made a mistake in giving it to me. Other people will have had to do much more for their Ph.D.s and therefore actually deserve it. I'll never be able to achieve anything meaningful in life.'

All or nothing: 'I can't even get up in the morning to get to a lecture on time, I'm just a complete failure.'

Generalization: 'I hate him. He said he would phone. I knew he didn't even like me. Nobody could ever love someone like me.'

Fortune teller error: 'I want to go to the disco. I know I won't enjoy it. No one will ever want to know me.'

Mind reading: 'She's never even spoken to me. But she always has that look on her face and I know she must hate me.'

Disqualifying the positive: 'But your grades are superb.' (counsellor) 'Anybody can be good at programming. I just can't do anything important.' (client)

As part of the assessment clients are provided with lists of such distortions and asked to check off their thinking as an awareness-raising exercise.

Typical student schemata

Schemata are templates which in effect summarize the way people have, from early experiences onward, made sense of their world. In information processing terms they act as stored sub-routines aiding quick interpretation of events, and even shape incoming data to conform to expectations. Nelson-Jones (1995) has a useful discussion of types. Schemata tend to be activated when an experience occurs similar to one earlier incorporated within the range of the template. Typical student schemata include:

- My worth is completely conditional on academic performance. (No identity other than an academic one.)
- I am utterly dependent on others for good feelings. (No valuing of personal experience, but gives away power by valuing the experience of everyone else thereby making the other an authority.)
- I must never be alone. (No dependable resources in me therefore must always have others around.)
- Everybody is always critical, therefore I'll never take anyone seriously. (Avoidance of meaningful personal relationships, and the sharing of subtle experience which goes with this, but an increased incidence of drunkenness, violence, promiscuity, etc.)

Strategy

The assessment leads directly to a formulation regarding the origin of the problem, maintenance factors, cognitive distortions, automatic thoughts and possible schemata. Even as this is being done the counsellor is educating the client into the model. The counsellor is active and directive. The counselling is focused on agreed objectives based on a now shared understanding of the model and how it applies to these specific problems. Although trust is important at first, it is made clear that as the client tests out the hypothesis, and discovers progress is being made, the more important factor is that the client begins to trust her own capacity to solve her own problems. It is made explicit that the client will increasingly become her own counsellor. The counsellor models surrogate information processing, and surrogate empathy which the client begins to apply to herself.

With students, one would typically have two sessions of an hour each within a week, then have gaps to enable homework to get done between further sessions. Each session is structured as follows:

- check how client is feeling;
- check homework and focus on ways of overcoming any difficulties;
- negotiate agenda for current session;
- work on refining understanding and capacity to identify and modify beliefs;
- agree new homework stemming directly from the current session;
- check on client experience of the session and correct any misunderstandings.

There are two basic approaches to changing cognitions: restructuring and Socratic dialogue. The former has been illustrated in the case of the Ph.D. student afraid to travel, the latter is close and detailed questioning and disputing. In short, one is enabling the client to identify ways and alternative ways to articulate self-narrative.

Techniques

Behavioural techniques such as graded exposure, relaxation and self-monitoring using forms, have already been illustrated. Other behavioural techniques are:

Scheduling: Particularly when working with the depressed, a list of activities to be fitted into a day at particular times can provide motivation and increase stimulation.

Behavioural experiments: Deliberate efforts to change behaviour in real situations, e.g. the Ph.D. student deliberately sitting in the Underground using new self-talk to see if relaxation techniques are even necessary.

Homework: Homework is crucial in that it emphasizes the experimental nature of the counselling through information-gathering and testing hypotheses. It also discourages dependency, putting the client on the road to practising self-counselling. It reinforces the counselling session discussions. It also reduces the number of formal sessions and their frequency while increasing the number of informal sessions the client is giving herself.

Cognitive techniques already mentioned include providing the client with a rationale for the approach, discussing why particular techniques are suggested and helping clients identify, examine and if necessary change cognitions. The dialogue in the section on assessment illustrates the standard 'downward arrow' technique: each client thought is assumed to be both 'true' and 'good' and one delves in further and further to unpack the underlying beliefs. Reattribution has also been illustrated. Other useful cognitive techniques may be found in Beck and Emery (1985) and include:

Perspective: The client is asked to role-play a friend and talk to the client, or just give the view of a close friend.

Counsel a friend: The client is asked to pretend a friend has the problem. What advice would they offer the friend?

Questioning: This is particularly useful when discussing illustrations of cognitive distortions on the forms issued to the clients:

'Are you really saying that you must, that it is always essential. . . . '
'If you must do that, does it follow that you have to be severely blamed for
    not doing it?'
'What is the evidence for. . . . '
'And the benefit to you of clinging to that view?'

A case of self harm

Susan cuts herself. She's been doing it for three years. She proudly displays
her wrist. She speaks of recently opening the scar again and again. Before
that she stubbed out cigarettes on her hands. She had also taken overdoses
of Paracetamol in the past. She's now completed her first few months at
university.

She describes how she thought she could escape at university, but it had
not made any difference. Now she's depressed. Her GP says she's not
clinically depressed and refers her for counselling.

The following transcript gives a taste of how the work progressed:

Counsellor: You seem angry. Perhaps you don't want to be here?
Client: No, it's not that. I'm just pissed off with Cynthia. She's my
                best friend. Was. She just told me to get lost.
Counsellor: Get lost?
Client: Says she wants space. I'm too intense. She can't cope with me.
                It's always the same. People always let you down, don't they?
                They pretend to care. You don't care either, not really. You
                just get paid to care.
Counsellor: You predict I too will let you down.
Client: Sure.
Counsellor: OK let's pause a moment to see if we can clarify the detail of
                what you are telling yourself.

It should be noted that, although relationship is the initial issue, the
underlying cognition may be expressed in the loose form 'I *must* do this as
it is the only way I can guarantee I will get taken *seriously*' (by both self and
others). The therapy does not focus directly on stopping self-harm. When
it has been sufficiently 'undermined' it will usually stop of its own accord.

The downward arrow technique was used to flush out underlying beliefs.
Susan went away to check out through homework monitoring whether
these identified beliefs were 'real' (all-pervasive) or not. She returned with
this summary:

To help me, to keep me safe, everyone must be perfect. They are not.

They should be. They must be. I can only be safe, bear it, if they are. I need now the set of perfect strong people my parents were or should have been when I was a kid. But I'm not a kid. I'm big and strong and I wasn't then. That's how my problem started. But now I maintain it by insisting I'm weak and they must be strong. They have to be. I must be a bad person otherwise those strong wise perfect people would love me perfectly. I really enjoy cutting myself. It's a moral imperative. The more the pain the better I am. The more worthy I am.

The therapy then focuses cognitively on restructuring around the related issues of 'must', 'worthiness' and 'seriously'. It also focuses behaviourally by the counsellor explicitly respecting the client's efforts in the counselling relationship and through homework in which 'worthiness' is gained through actions which promote self-respect, and generalize to other-respect. Later the issues of 'perfect' and 'non-perfect' attributions for people are explored with the associated meanings 'safe' and 'vulnerable'. Babiker and Arnold (1997) provide a helpful overview of such issues.

Summary

In student counselling the structure of CBT enables it quickly to focus the work on the crucial issues underlying what are often confused presentations of a problem. It uses homework to train clients to be counsellors to themselves, empowering them with emotional resilience for the future at minimal cost. The educational context makes essential some adaptations to normal CBT clinical practice, the most important of which is providing emotional support.

Bibliography

Babiker, G. and Arnold, L. (1997) *The Language of Injury: Comprehending Self-mutilation*, Leicester: The British Psychological Society: 137.
Bandura, A. (1982) 'Self-efficacy mechanisms in human agency', *American Psychologist*, 37: 122–47.
Beck, A.T. and Emery, G. (1985) *Anxiety Disorders and Phobias: a Cognitive Perspective*, New York: Basic Books.
Beck, A.T., Freeman, A. and associates (1990) *Cognitive Therapy of Personality Disorders*, New York: Guilford Press.
Beck, A.T., Rush, A.J., Shaw, B.F. and Emery, G. (1979) *Cognitive Therapy of Depression*, New York: Wiley.
Benoit, D. and Parker, K. (1994) 'Stability and transmission of attachment across three generations', *Child Development*, 65: 1444–56.
Dryden, W. (1990) *Rational-Emotive Counselling in Action*, London: Sage.

Ellis, A. (1962) *Reason and Emotion in Psychotherapy*, New York: Lyle Stuart.

Fonagy, P., Steele, M., Steele, H., Higgitt, A. and Target, M. (1994) 'The theory and practice of resilience', *Journal of Child Psychology and Psychiatry*, 35: 231–57.

Hall, J.N. and Baker, R.D. (1986) 'Token economies and schizophrenia: a review' in A. Kerr and R.P. Snaith (eds), *Contemporary Issues in Schizophrenia*, London: Gaskell.

Hawton, K., Salkovskis, P.M., Kirk, J. and Clark, D. (1989) *Cognitive Behaviour Therapy for Psychiatric Problems: a Practical Guide*, Oxford: Oxford Medical Publications.

Holmes, J. (1997) 'Attachment, autonomy, intimacy: some clinical implications of attachment theory', *British Journal of Medical Psychology*, 70: 231–48.

Howard, K.I., Kopta, S.M., Krause, M.S. and Orlinsky, D.E. (1986) 'The dose-effect relationship in psychotherapy', *American Psychologist*, 41: 159–64.

Kazdin, A.E. (1978), *History of Behavior Modification: Experimental Foundations of Contemporary Research*, Baltimore: University Park Press.

Kohut, H. (1984) *How does Analysis Cure?* ed. A. Goldberg with P.E. Stepansky, Chicago: University of Chicago Press.

Koss, M.P. and Shiang, J. (1994) 'Research on brief psychotherapy', in A.E. Bergin and S.L. Garfield (eds), *Handbook of Psychotherapy and Behavior Change* (4th edn) New York: Wiley: 664–700.

Lindsay, S.J.E. and Powell, G.E. (1994) *The Handbook of Clinical Adult Psychology* (2nd edn) London: Routledge.

Main, M. (1995) 'Recent studies in attachment: overview, with selected implications for clinical work', in S. Goldberg, R. Muir and J. Kerr (eds), *Attachment Theory: Social, Developmental and Clinical Perspectives*, New York: Academic Press.

Meichenbaum, D.H. (1975) 'Self-instructional methods', in F.H. Kanfer and A.P. Goldstein (eds), *Helping People Change: a Textbook of Methods*, New York: Pergamon Press: 357–91.

Nelson-Jones, R. (1995) *The Theory and Practice of Counselling*, London: Cassell.

Parry, G. (1996) *NHS Psychotherapy Services in England – Review of Strategic Policy*, London: NHS Executive: 47–54.

Rist, J.M. (1978) 'The stoic concept of detachment', in J.M. Rist (ed.), *The Stoics*, Berkeley: University of California Press.

Roth, A.D. and Fonagy, P. (1996) *What Works for Whom? A Critical Review of Psychotherapy Research*, New York: Guilford Press.

Scott, M.J. and Dryden, W. (1996) 'The cognitive-behavioural paradigm', in R. Woolfe and W. Dryden (eds), *Handbook of Counselling Psychology*, London: Sage: Chapter 7.

Tillich, P. (1969) *The Courage to Be*, London: Fontana: 20–7.

Wolpe, J. (1982) *The Practice of Behavior Therapy* (3rd edn), New York: Pergamon Press.

7 Establishing group psychotherapy in a student counselling service

Peter Mark and Gabrielle Rifkind

Establishing a group in a new setting

In September 1995, we were appointed as group analysts in a university counselling and psychotherapy section of student services. We were both employed two days a week throughout the whole year. Such an appointment reflected a shift in culture in this institution and potentially in others. While groups had already been run at the university for students by individually trained therapists, there was recognition that a service needed to be developed that deepened the culture and traditions in this area and provided a more extensive resource.

Upon appointment we began to talk to fellow group analysts who had worked in university settings. Gone was our initial zest for the job. They were to tell us that college groups were essentially problematic. Students were often too unreliable to sustain group culture. They could only make a commitment week by week. There were problematic confidentiality issues and many students were too self-conscious to talk in groups. However, in spite of our feelings of initial disillusionment, one of us would carry the spirit of hope allowing the other to express the doubts. We were pretty clear, however, that we would not communicate any of our ambivalence to our colleagues. While they had the courage to appoint us and had shown a firm commitment to establishing group work, we did not want to sow any seeds of doubt for them. We knew that individually trained practitioners, however much they supported groups, fundamentally preferred an individual course of treatment, with groups felt to be second best, a compromise. We had no wish to reinforce this thinking and our task was to convince our colleagues and ourselves of the efficacy of groups in this setting, and the importance of offering treatment best suited to the student.

The setting

On our arrival we were introduced to the group room, which comprised an ill assortment of chairs, heavily stained carpet and Blu Tack on the walls. A huge computer terminal system sat aggressively against one of the walls. Our boss sensed our disappointment and quickly demonstrated her masterful negotiation of the bureaucracy, managing to procure some funding for the painting of the room and the purchasing of some new furniture. Her responsiveness was much appreciated and we purchased nine fresh wicker chairs (£25 each), some lively bright cushions and a cheerful rug. The sum total of our expenditure was £280. We emphasize the detail because communicating care about your environment to group members will often translate to a feeling of being taken seriously and does not require huge financial resources. We wanted to communicate respect, responsibility, warmth, containment and safety in the construction of the environment.

Group analysts spend a lot of time on what is called 'dynamic administration' – essentially a commitment to the setting. Like all counsellors and psychotherapists, we have to protect our environment, ensure that there are no telephones ringing, no knocks on the doors and a private space where voices cannot be overheard. In addition we need nine similar chairs, comfy enough to sit on for an hour and a half. Nevertheless, group analysts do not believe in the spirit of blank walls or screens. The room we have adapted is hopefully both welcoming and pleasing to the eye, perhaps standing in contrast to much of institutional life.

Selection

Our first task was to get sufficient referrals to establish groups. In an NHS setting or in private practice timing is not so critical, as one expects to take about three to six months to set up a group. In the university setting, because of the academic year, there is pressure to establish a group as soon as possible.

To assemble a group of eight probably requires interviewing twice as many referrals. The aim is to establish a group with a healthy mix of similarities and differences. One tries to avoid 'isolates', for example one black student, one lone man, a lone woman who has been sexually abused, etc. In establishing a range of emotional communication in the group, it is very helpful to have at least one member who can express anger, with perhaps somebody else who is more on the depressive end of the spectrum. We try to balance someone who talks too much with someone who has great difficulty in finding words, a student who always projects the blame on to others and the victim who always takes the blame back on to him or herself. Over time one hopes that this rich pot-pourri will create a 'matrix' in which the different bits of each individual will get mixed up in the group. The angry members of the group will be able to become more reflective and the deeply depressed group members will have more access to their anger. Similarly the projectors will have an opportunity to re-own their projections and the introjectors will become more aware of the role they play in carrying the projections of others.

However, all this is partly an ideal. It becomes closer to reality when one has a range of groups available and thus can place potential group members accordingly. In the early days of setting up groups in this setting we did not feel we had this luxury. Timing was also critical. The student term began in October, and in order to establish the group we wanted to give ourselves at least six sessions before the Christmas holiday. In practice this meant starting with groups as small as four. Ideally we wanted to balance gender and to have a range of ages.

Group or individual: dilemmas of assessment

Most people who present themselves for therapy imagine themselves in dyadic, personal relationships. The unconscious image may be of the mother–child relationship in perfect attunement where they will be effortlessly understood. A group in contrast may stir up anxieties about fighting for space, conflict, violence, struggling with difference with people you may not like and the potential shame of talking in front of others. Not a very inviting prospect. It is certainly true that the group environment may be more unpredictable, may involve more conflict and less attunement. It will also be closer to real life, and the relationships people create outside the group may well be re-enacted in this imperfect group environment.

However, the group, while it may sometimes be demanding and difficult, may also offer the opportunity for profound shared experiences. So the young woman who feels unbearable shame about being sexually abused, or the young man who has to share the humiliation of having been bullied and unable to defend himself at school, may for the first time have the experience of not being alone in his or her shame. There is a shared common experience, with the longer-term possibility of members being able to respond differently because of a shift in how they feel about themselves and a consequent maturing in their outside relationships as they learn a deeper perspective from other group members about the 'difficult' conflictual viewpoint of the 'other'. Groupwork offers a unique mirroring potential with direct feedback. Students often yearn to increase their sense of how they are seen by others. Such feedback is seldom available in individual therapy and groups offer the opportunity to increase awareness of the gap between how one sees oneself and how one is seen by others.

Despite this, the reality remains that most people presenting themselves for counselling or therapy will often initially resist the idea of a group. The thought of talking in front of others will seem frightening. They will be surprised by the suggestion and will wish for the intimacy of the one-to-one relationship. They might say that they don't think that the group is a good idea because it feels difficult. In practice, one might respond as the therapist by saying that this might be the very reason why it might be a good idea. Slowly, as one begins to talk about the group, there is often a shift in response. The idea of a group becomes both simultaneously exciting and frightening. It would be true to say that there is some correlation between the therapist's communication about groups and how far he or she really believes in them and the likelihood of the student perceiving that it is a real option for them. If the counsellor communicates her own ambivalence about the effectiveness of groups, this will clearly influence whether students are able to consider it as a real option for themselves. Conversely, it is important not to 'push' the student into the wrong setting, and it is a matter of training and experience to know when the assessee's resistance indicates individual therapy as the treatment of choice. However, while students need to be able to manage the intimacy of the one-to-one relationship, they also need to be able to manage groups. Much of their learning takes place in groups, as do many of their social relationships. One of the crucial tasks for these young people is how to find a sense of self in the group; to find a voice and to know oneself as a separate person with one's own thoughts and not to be overwhelmed by group culture. They need to develop a sense of intimacy within the small group also and this involves the need to develop a sufficiently secure identity to resist the power of the group when necessary.

Clearly some students do need individual therapy at the point of presenting for help. Or they might need some individual work before they are ready for the group. This combination can be extremely helpful and some individual sessions can make a very useful preparation for the group.

Being in a group helps them develop a language to express themselves. Some young people who present themselves to the counselling service have developmentally lacked good enough one-to-one relationships and this might be what they require. They may come from a large family where they have always had to compete for attention or have been parented in such a way that their own experience has never been attended to.

Some students on assessment are very difficult to listen to. The counter-transference is so strong that it evokes very negative feelings in the therapist. The group can often be a place where individual relationships are not so intense and there is a dilution of how they are experienced, and therefore such members can feel safer, more contained by the group.

Establishing the culture

There are different aspects to establishing group culture, including the wider culture of the institution, the team in which one works and the group itself. Ideally one hopes to establish a culture within the wider institution where teaching staff are aware of the usefulness of groups as a resource for students when dealing with emotional difficulties. In practice, we cannot yet claim to have been entirely successful at this institutional level. With colleagues, however, it has been crucially important to increase awareness of groups as a resource.

Our team is made up of psychotherapists, counsellors, a psycho-analytically trained psychiatrist and the welfare officers. We have a weekly meeting at which allocations are made and students causing concern are discussed. This is a useful and appropriate meeting in which to increase colleagues' awareness of groups as a potential resource. Colleagues have concerns, not always voiced, about groupwork. They may think of groups as at times out of control, or there may be worries about confidentiality, especially in the college setting, or there may be a belief that the one-to-one relationship provides more potential for containment and in-depth work. We find it useful to keep groups on the meeting agenda, clarifying why a group might be helpful for particular students. There is no doubt that in our department there has been a significant culture shift as a result of being better informed. This coincides with a genuine sense of goodwill towards groups, and a commitment to co-operative teamwork.

Perhaps the most crucial element though is the establishing of the culture within the therapy groups themselves. With each group we aim to encourage the development of a culture where it is safe to discuss aspects of students' lives, or issues where they have previously felt silenced, often because of shame or embarrassment. In the process the student can transform from inhibited self-conscious communication to a degree of emotional literacy, or as Pines (1986) describes it, from cohesive to coherent communication.

For some students this may involve becoming familiar with a new language that gives them an opportunity to describe their interior world and share this with others. We do not teach them a language, but, as the culture of the group emerges, members become more familiar with the language of intimate relationships and handling differences. Over time they discover that there are ways of handling conflict that do not have to involve either avoidance or a fight. Examples of this will be detailed later in the chapter.

Preparation for the group

In the individual assessment sessions students are told about the rules, boundaries and expectations of the group, as follows:

*   They are expected to attend each session and if they cannot it is expected that a message will be left for the group. It is useful to point out to them at this point that, if therapy is to work, they will need to know each other's stories and missing a session is problematic and will inhibit the development of the whole group. They may have little awareness of this in the early stages as they may well believe that their contribution is of little consequence. It is also useful at this stage to point out the difference between the impact of missing a group session and missing an individual session. An individual session only affects the relationship between the individual and the therapist, whereas missing a group actually impacts on several other people.
*   We would also talk about the expectation that group members do not meet outside the group. While this is particularly difficult in a university or college setting, we emphasize that for therapy groups to work effectively it is important to hold this boundary. If one does not there is the potential for sub-groups to emerge which can challenge the working culture of a therapy group, not to mention the exploitation of the therapeutic setting by the formation of sexual relationships outside the group.
*   We would also wish to talk to group members about how they might at some point wish to drop out of the group. They would probably move between feelings of idealization of the group to sometimes feeling it turgid and difficult, leaving them wondering why they were there. It would be at those moments that it becomes vital that they do not 'act out' but find a way of thinking about this in the group. In our experience, group members who changed were the ones who found a way of struggling through these difficult moments.
*   We would also try and establish some culture around notions of leaving, building the idea of a good ending into the beginning. We suggest that if a student were thinking of leaving the group, it would be important to explore with other group members the meaning of their desire, and their readiness, to leave. This boundary in practice can be very difficult to establish in shorter-term groups.

Adapting to the institution

As group analysts we are trained to run 'stranger' groups on a long-term basis, where the culture can be built up over time. This is not always realistic in a university setting, and whilst we run one postgraduate group where the members mostly live locally, the majority of students are there for two twelve-week terms and one six-week term in summer.

We therefore have to adapt our working methods to be responsive to these conditions. We cannot assume that group culture will be sustained over the years or that we will have more than one academic year to work with students. The implications for the groups are that we have to be more proactive in these short-term groups. It is not necessarily appropriate to wait for material to present itself. Sometimes it is more helpful actively to shape the process. In such brief groups it is often important to be more focused and actively engaged in naming the conflicts often just beneath the surface. It is also necessary to hold the end in sight right from the beginning. This helps to focus the issue of time more sharply, and students need to take responsibility for how they use the limited time.

In a university setting we cannot truly establish a 'stranger' culture. While we try not to have students in the same year or course in the same group, we have to retain a degree of flexibility around these issues. Students are likely to meet each other along the corridors of the institution. While we state clearly that we don't encourage the developing of any relationships during the life of the group, we don't expect group members coldly to ignore each other outside the group. However, it is necessary to raise issues and feelings about such meetings in the group at regular intervals; to ignore them can lead to sudden crises.

Why psychotherapy groups work in a university or college setting

We need to acknowledge that the university or college finances a counselling service in order to support the primary aim of assisting young people to study and pass their examinations. It is, however, our belief that the more integrated the students are into university or college life, the more able they are to handle relationships, and the greater awareness they have of themselves in these relationships, the more likely they will be able to sustain their experience and be effective. Some young people do, however, put all their energies into studying, and turn up first-class degrees, perhaps at the cost of developing their relationships.

When students present themselves to us for help, they are usually not in the first instance coming for psychotherapy. They are presenting themselves because their lives are in sufficient distress that they are unable to function well enough in their personal and college life. Whatever symptoms they present, their difficulties invariably express themselves in relationship problems. It is in this context that the psychotherapy group is able to provide an arena for young people to explore how they experience themselves in relationships and how they are experienced by others. They may present with panic attacks, eating disorders, depression, past experiences of family breakdown or having been bullied. The relationship difficulties might well be intensified by leaving home and starting further education; increasing their potential to feel isolated, to spend long periods of time alone, to have a poor sense of self and to believe that they have very little to offer in relationships. This immediately recreates itself in the group in the form of a cautiousness about speaking, or of feeling what they say is worthless and that it is better to be silent; that they are entitled neither to be heard nor to be responded to.

In one of our first groups, two members related painful experiences of being severely bullied at school. Consequently they had learnt to maintain silence, to keep their often fearful and angry thoughts inside, and when they forced themselves to speak they exuded tension, releasing words in a nervous, stuttering way. The whole group initially took on this form of communication. Similarity was all too evident, but enough healthy difference appeared to be lacking. The group dilemma was unblocked with the introduction of a young woman into the group. She was able to be more direct in her challenges and to break through the tentative nature of the group, facilitating a change in this initial culture.

Such a crucial membership addition provides an example of the advantage the 'slow–open' groupwork model has over the more closed, fixed-term group. The complex factors involved in establishing a therapeutic 'group matrix' often involve great time and effort. Inevitably some members will leave at the end of term, but careful management often allows a core group to survive out of term periods, to be strengthened again with the new student intake.

The group as microcosm

The group can be seen as a microcosm of relationships outside. For example, a group member who is timid and fearful of the impact he has on others is likely to recreate this tentative approach in the group. Another group member, who is more bullying in his communication and has difficulty in listening to others, will act similarly in the group. The difference, however, is that the group can become like a glass house, where people can look in, reflect upon and analyse their relationships with one another, something seldom done in the world outside. This helps members to increase their capacity to empathize. Many bring narcissistic ways of communicating, with self-absorption blocking openness to others. A well-functioning group will quickly offer the opportunity to develop attunement to others. Individuals will begin to explore their own internal lives, their anxieties, fears, doubts and positive feelings, as well as feelings of self-contempt, and how they imagine they are seen by others. Over time they will be able to differentiate between their own perception of themselves and how they interact and are thereby experienced by other group members.

The group also offers the potential for each member to tell and retell their stories as a way of making sense of their experiences and reducing their sense of isolation and shame. This is particularly true in areas such as sexual abuse, bullying and eating problems. The sharing and connecting with others becomes part of the therapeutic process. Over time the group finesses a language for communication in which members are able to make themselves understood and to understand others. Many enter groups expecting that their experience will be understood; without verbalizing it, they hope the group will instantly be a perfectly attuned mother. Much frustration lies in the area of feeling misunderstood but not knowing how to be understood. This may be due to a paucity of emotional language to describe their experience or to an inability to see the correlation between intimate communication and being understood.

Gradually learning to find a voice leads to an increase in the individual sense of self. By differentiating self from others, students learn what they think and feel in the face of others. The experience offers the possibility of being part of the group but also having a separate sense of self within the group, having reached the point of internal cohesion where the individual can tolerate similarities and differences and have an autonomous sense of self that is also connected to others. This coherent sense of self includes the possibility of integrating many aspects of the self including a destructive self, a creative self, a cultural self and a private self. In effect we aim to provide each with an experience of becoming 'more fully oneself in reciprocity with others' (Brown 1994: 80).

The group as family

A very useful way of seeing the therapy group is as a 'corrective recapitulation of the primary family group' (Yalom). There is a clear link between what the students bring from their social interaction outside and how they interact in the group, and these patterns emerge largely from early family interaction. Members begin to face immediately issues around competition, rivalry, getting heard and giving and taking space; furthermore, authority feelings quickly emerge towards the conductor.

The therapy group offers a rich arena for studying this behaviour, as each individual finds their own way to cope with the challenge of the group. Although we work only with 'stranger' groups there are many parallels with family work, as pointed out by Behr (1994: 78).

> Both stranger group therapy and family therapy take the individual from isolation to communication, from telling the story of the symptom to telling the story of its meanings. In both types of group, the individual members listen to each other, helped along by the therapist and the setting. . . . The symptom and its effects are ultimately shared by the whole group, translated into communicable language and dispersed in the group matrix.

Group therapy widens the interactional context of the parent–child dyad of individual therapy. Although the baby's earliest experiences go on within the intensity of the dyadic relationship with the mother, it is worth emphasizing that motherhood also implies fatherhood: even in the pre-Oedipal phase the relationship is not exclusively mother and baby, and the mother communicates to the baby her own relationship with the father, the outside world and maybe also her other children. The infant normally grasps very quickly that it is not the sole object for the mother but part of an interactive system.

Christine, a narcissistically preoccupied 22-year-old struggling academically and with a history of drug overdoses, was referred to the group after extended individual assessment. The referring therapist felt that her obsessional, competitive envy towards her younger sister (20) and sense of grievance against her parents would be more effectively addressed in the open feedback of the group setting. Predictably, Christine immediately voiced her family grievances with an abundance of stories, all with her in the victim role. She was unable to listen to the group members' initial tentative comments, unless they expressed the sought-after sympathy which would reinforce her victim position. After two sessions of this, the group quite understandably became impatient. Some were switching off and some voiced feelings perhaps akin to those of Christine's other family members, connected with a feeling that Christine showed no corresponding interest in their material. Gradually more direct and forceful feedback emerged to Christine than would normally be possible between therapist and patient early in the dyadic setting.

Ian:	(*irritated*) You're always going on about what your sister does to you but we never hear what you contribute to the fights. When I fight with my girlfriend there's always two sides, two ways to look at it.
Christine:	(*taken aback*) But that's not fair. You don't know her. She's not like your girlfriend. She's impossible. Just last night. . . .
Conductor:	Could I stop you there, Christine, because I think it would help us move forward if we knew what others felt about what Ian has just said. (*tense silence*)
Conductor:	It may feel difficult to voice anything other than sympathetic words to Christine. Maybe we fear she won't be able to handle them or might leave the group.
Christine:	(*quickly*) Oh no, I like it here. Everyone, feel free to say what you like to me. I don't care.
Ann:	(*who has been most clearly angry and withdrawn because of Christine's dominance*) Far from it all being your sister's fault, I think you're probably pretty hard to live with too.
Christine:	(*hurt*) That's not fair, you don't understand what goes on in my house.
Conductor:	That is true, all any of us can go on is how we experience each other in here. Would it help you, Christine, to hear why Ann said what she did?
Christine:	I don't care. As I said, everyone's entitled to their own opinion. There's no reason why it should bother me.
Ann:	You take up all the time in this group. No one else gets a word in edgeways. If you're like that at home, no wonder there's fights all the time.
Christine:	That's not my fault. If I didn't speak in here, you lot would all sit around like dummies. I'm doing the group a favour by giving you something to focus on, and now I'm attacked

	for it. Well, okay then, I'll shut up and leave some other sucker to take the shit.
Ann:	You'd do us all a favour if you did keep quiet.
Conductor:	What's going on? What do you all think is happening now?
John:	(*anxious*) It doesn't feel safe in here.
Conductor:	Right now I agree, and we need to think together so we can be helpful and not destructive.
	(*tense silence*)
Conductor:	What I feel has happened is that we are witnessing Christine replaying her conflicts with her sister in here.
Christine:	(*to Ann*) Yeah, you remind me a bit of her. That's just how she wipes me out.
Conductor:	And now we have the chance to think about it and not just react or run away.

As the group goes on to unravel the process over the following sessions, much productive material emerges, about family conflicts, the hurt and the resolution. Some months later Christine remains in the group and, while still more comfortable in her victim position, has changed in her use of the group. She no longer dominates, but chooses her moments and expresses herself in a more shared communication, no longer separate and cut off, but relating her material to group themes and developing perspective and sensitivity about how she impacts on others. Our expectation would be that this new 'sibling interaction' in the group will begin to manifest itself therapeutically in her difficulties with family and sibling groups outside.

In the university and college setting, students bring many family issues to work on in the group, consciously and unconsciously. A very common theme is separation anxiety, as members talk about thoughts and feelings around leaving home. This is particularly acute for undergraduates in their first year, who can benefit greatly from the mix with more mature students, who may have succeeded in putting more distance between themselves and their families. The combination of first-hand recent experience and advice-giving, alongside the more reflective stance of the therapist, can be remarkably potent in moving students along developmentally. Some students begin with a lack of awareness that their puzzling symptoms (often panic attacks) can have anything to do with separation from home, and the experience of others comes as a major revelation.

The resolution of such individual conflicts, using the group, comes through the very process of being together, of moving closer towards intimate sharing. Students missing the security of home, or even those from dysfunctional families, guilty and fearful about deserting their role of keeping the family together, often experience their early days in further education as disappointing, superficial and alienating. More intimate relationships seem impossible. The group engages them in the process of relating on a deep level without the boundaryless risks of life 'outside' and prepares them for making more meaningful relationships when they feel ready. Much material emerges about being parentified children, or having squabbling parents, or leaving younger siblings behind, along with the common fears of not being up to parental expectations academically.

So individuals bring both their past and present into each group, and it is the conductor's job to help the members understand this and begin to work with its potential. Group analysis, in its overlap with systems theory, provides the framework for relating internal objects to external relationships.

Transference in the group

The group presents the opportunity to work on transferential relationships which go beyond the dyadic focus on the analyst. The analytic group provides multiple transference possibilities with a variety of shifting transferences. Of course, only a small percentage of these can ever be consciously taken up and worked with, but the conductor or co-therapists need to be alive to this complexity. For some, the group becomes homogenized into a single transference figure represented by the circle: this may often be seen as an intrusive mother, while the therapist becomes the boundary-holding father. The therapeutic aim is to help the members differentiate, relate to others as individuals, re-own projections and see with increasing degrees of reality. Unlike one-to-one therapy, when the main transference open to analysis is parental, the group offers a wider canvas of sibling transference, often but not always less deeply felt than parental distortions.

As with other aspects of group therapy, members are given a less passive role than is usual in one-to-one work in actively challenging each other's perceptions and making the transference links, sometimes even pointing out the conductor's counter-transference. The therapist's inappropriate intervention is often more openly manifest in the group, as the members have the protection of numbers against analytic misinterpretation and potential exploitation. A higher level of personal transparency is often necessary in the group therapist, and this links to the fact that therapeutic outcome in groups is less dependent on transference resolution.

There are several other equally important therapeutic factors in group psychotherapy. The therapist's primary task is to encourage their development, specifically the move towards a cohesive group matrix. Knowing when to focus transference material on to oneself and when to turn it back to group interaction is critical. In our experience the development of the group in the earlier stages is considerably enhanced by focusing on the 'sibling' interactions. Only rarely would we actively induce the transference on to ourselves, as in situations of a high degree of conflict in the group, or where there is a danger of someone being scapegoated. On these occasions, hostile feelings can be more safely directed on to the conductor (where they more probably belong). A more mature group, once the matrix is well established, can do productive analytic work on transference feelings towards the conductor. The therapist's awareness of the counter-transference is just as important for the group analyst as for those working one-to-one, and again contains more potential for complexity.

Gina has been engaged in what she feels is a battle with the female co-conductor of her group for a year, reflecting and graphically illustrating her presenting problem, which is extreme conflict with her tutor, and the link to earlier unresolved parental issues. When the group conductors attempted to make these links and help Gina work on the problem, she became angry and sought to establish a similarly conflicted relationship with the female conductor, characterized by her ambivalent desire to get close to the conductor and at the same time attack her. She had got into difficulties with her tutor by expecting her to provide the warm, personal relationship she couldn't have with her mother, and found herself re-enacting a similar kind of relationship. With the group conductor she expected another distant, misunderstanding and withdrawn relationship, and worked hard to fit her experience of therapeutic boundaries into this template.

This began to change following one group session:

Gina: . . . but I suppose you (*to the female conductor*) will see this as all to do with my mother, yet again.

Conductor: I was wondering how *you* see it.

Gina: Well, I don't think you appreciate just how frustrating it is to . . . (*goes on to relate her feelings about being infantilized by her tutor's insensitivity*).

Conductor: You may be right there. I haven't paid enough attention to just how frustrating that must be in its own right, and to your experience that my seeing it in the context of your relationship with your mother in some way discounts your anger and frustration.

This freed Gina to do her own analytic work on the feelings, and represented a turning point in the transference with the conductor. While at times this continued to be conflicted, it no longer prevented Gina from using her considerable psychological insight to help others in the group instead of trying to outwit the conductor.

Conclusion

Group psychotherapy is now widely established, and extensive research studies show it to be a highly effective treatment for a wide variety of psychological disorders. In this chapter we have tried to focus on some of the practical and theoretical reasons why groups can be so effective in the context of university and college counselling services, based on our own experience.

We have also attempted to emphasize the need to adapt the group analytic method to the setting. This may involve a need to be more flexible concerning the long-term 'slow–open' model. Many student groups will be briefer, and more closed, working within the limitations of the college terms. Consequently the therapist at times needs to be more focused and directive without detracting from the central task for the group of building up its own identity. At times, specific issues related to this setting – such as separation anxiety, study difficulties, intense fears around failure and/or success, first serious sexual commitments, alcohol and drug experimentation – will throw an individual in the group into sudden crisis, with a real danger of suicide. Group therapists need to pay close attention and be prepared to offer additional one-to-one sessions whenever necessary, reintegrating the material back into the group wherever possible. Nevertheless, we have found the fundamental principle of the group analytic method to be well suited to these groups, and we have attempted to relate some of our personal experience of establishing an effective groupwork culture within the institution, the counselling service, and in each of our student psychotherapy groups.

Bibliography

Ashback, C. and Schermer, V. (1994) *Object Relations, the Self and the Group*, London: Routledge.

Behr, H. (1994) 'Families and Group Analysis', in D. Brown and L. Zinkin (eds), *The Psyche and the Social World*, London: Routledge.

Brown, D. and Zinkin, L. (eds) (1994) *The Psyche and the Social World – Developments in Group Analytical Theory*, London: Routledge.

Pines, M. (1986) 'Coherency and its disruption in the development of the self', *British Journal of Psychotherapy*, 2(3): 180–5.

Yalom, I. and Vinogradov, S. (1987) *Group Psychotherapy*, Washington: American Psychiatric Press.

Wolfe, E. (1988) *Treating The Self: Elements of Clinical Psychology*, New York: Guilford Press.

8 Issues of difference in further and higher education

Colin Lago and Nigel Humphrys

Introduction

Changes in the student body within British higher education have been enormous over the last thirty years. This diversity can clearly be seen by comparing the findings of the Robbins report in the early 1960s and the recent Dearing report.

In the early 1960s, one person in eighteen entered full-time higher education. Today, the figure is one in three. There were barely 200,000 students in full-time higher education in 1962–3; in 1996–7, there are 1.1 million with 500,000 on part-time HE courses, and 200,000 in FE colleges.

This huge increase has partly been achieved by the recruitment of students from areas previously underrepresented. Women, who made up only 26 per cent of students in higher education in the early 1960s, now account for 51 per cent, although they still remain underrepresented in the postgraduate sector and in science and technology. A most important change over the last thirty years has been the substantial increase in mature students from 41 per cent in 1962–3 to 58 per cent in 1995–6. Over 30 per cent of the student population is now over the age of 30. Four per cent of all students are from Access courses. There has also been a significant rise in the numbers of ethnic minority students recruited into HE.

Given the above population changes, the question is, have the university and college systems changed to take account of this? It appears not. While only one in ten under-21-year-olds believed that their needs were not being catered for, 47 per cent of students aged 25 and over felt that not enough thought was given to the needs of mature students. It seems from this that universities and colleges are still very much geared towards the school-leaver in terms of their organization and structure.

From the counselling point of view, the question is how far our services have come in providing meaningful and appropriate services to the complete range of students now in higher education, particularly those whom we very reluctantly term 'different' for the purposes of this chapter.

Difference and diversity

The definition of difference itself has presented us with particular semantic, philosophical, emotional, psychological and sociological challenges. These have proved difficult to resolve satisfactorily. What does difference mean in terms of students? Different from whom? Different to what? The definition of what constitutes difference implies a particular dominant norm against which such difference is measured. For example, we have already cited that 51 per cent of the student population is presently female. The slightly smaller percentage, therefore, of the national male student population implies they may be described as one of the 'different' groups. Later in the chapter we cite one university with a 75 per cent mature student population. The population of traditional students (18–21-year-olds) has dominated as the normative reference model. In this particular university they are distinctly in the minority!

Difference, therefore, becomes associated with the following ranges of criteria:

majority	—	minority
male	—	female
powerful	—	powerless
wealth	—	poverty
resourced	—	under-resourced
supported	—	unsupported
able-bodied	—	disabled

Inevitably, the 'sociological' criteria of class, nationality, culture of origin, disability, gender, sexual identity, sexual preference and poverty have played a considerable part in our consideration of this term, which often is used as an ascription carrying negative connotations.

From the above examples we are keen, therefore, not to project onto any group or individual the title of 'different' as a pejorative concept. Difference is a relational concept. Salt is different to sugar. Both are different to each other. To have differences is perfectly valid. When differences become loaded with social judgements, often with negative values, we become concerned with their effect upon those so ascribed.

Differences are not deficiencies, they are just differences. Differences are relative, not absolute. Spectrums of difference in all things human therefore cover wide ranges of attitudes, beliefs and behaviours. The counsellor, under pressure, will often have to hang on to these concepts of relativity. One of the main tasks in the personal and professional development of counsellors is to achieve a deep appreciation of their own stereotypes and prejudices and their own psychological limits in working with difference. In this way, they may be better equipped to respond both to individuals in distress and to institutional incidents that cause anxiety and stress.

In recent years, American discussions of these phenomena have focused on the term 'diversity'. For the purposes of this chapter we appreciate this notion of 'diversity' as one that symbolizes the equal validity of a whole range of students attending higher education.

Later sections in the chapter feature discussions of particular groups of students (and there are several significant groups we have not had space to consider), but these are written with the above concerns in mind, and therefore with an underpinning philosophy of equality in diversity.

We have taken a somewhat serious view in this chapter on the impact of 'differentness' and its resultant implications for individual experience. This was inevitable, given the many clients who have suffered because of their 'differentness'. However, we are also aware of the great value of students who may be seen as 'different' for their friends, their studies and their educational environment. For this reason, among many others, those that are 'different' are worthy of social and educational support, for they often have unique capacities that may transpire to be of great service to themselves and society.

Issues of difference

The self and identity transformation

Students in higher education who hail from non-traditional, under-represented, disenfranchised or 'socially discriminated against' groups may not only have to contend with the general transitional issues faced by all students in higher education, but also have to engage with social processes and relations that are particular to them and their situations.

The last decade in the United States has seen an extensive development in the use of models describing ethnic identity development. These models have been constructed to (approximately) describe a series of stages of development that individuals may move through in terms of their awareness of self and how their self relates to other groups in society. In broad terms, the models hypothesize that belonging to a majority group in society will result in a very different sense of identity and capacity for relationship to other groups than that of someone who hails from a minority group.

These models have now been developed, through extensive research, for a range of different ethnic groups in the USA as well as for the dominant majority. The general ideas contained by these models are helpful in considering the stages of development the higher education experience exposes all students to. We therefore provide simplified examples below.

	White Racial Consciousness Model (Helms 1984)	Minority Identity Development Model (Atkinson *et al.* 1989)
Stage 1	*Contact*: unawareness of self as a racial being, tendency to ignore differences.	*Conformity*: identifies more with dominant group values. Negative attitudes are exhibited towards self and others of same ethnic group.
Stage 2	*Disintegration*: involves becoming aware of racism leading to guilt, depression and negative feelings.	*Dissonance*: Experiences confusion and conflict about previously held views and values. Becomes aware of issues involving racism, sexism, oppression, etc.
Stage 3	*Reintegration*: typified by hostility towards minorities and positive bias towards one's own group.	*Resistance and immersion*: involves active rejection and distrust of the dominant culture and greater identification with their own. May become active in challenging oppression.
Stage 4	*Pseudo-independence*: increasing interest in racial group similarities and differences accompanied by intellectual acceptance of others.	*Introspection*: involves a questioning of the rigid rejection of the dominant group's values resulting in experiences of conflict and confusion regarding loyalty to one's own group.

continued . . .

Stage 5	*Autonomy*: acceptance of racial differences and similarities with appreciation and respect. Active seeking of cross-racial encounters.	*Synergetic articulation – and awareness*: represents a stage of resolution of the above conflicts and offers a sense of fulfilment regarding personal cultural identity.

These models offer potential analogies to the processes of personal identity change that new students are inevitably exposed to, by virtue of their being students. Like other psychological models applied to different human experiences (e.g. culture shock, bereavement, etc.) there are: (1) no guarantees that everyone passes through all stages; (2) no time limits set on the duration of stages; and (3) the complexity of human beings set against the relative simplicity of the models means that some students may simultaneously experience two or three stages. However, the use of well-researched models like these can throw light on students' experiences, raising questions such as:

- What happens to a student's identity in relation to others when they engage in further or higher education?
- What happens to a 'minority' student's identity in relation to others in the dominant majority when they engage in further or higher education?
- If the process of identity formation and change is particularly 'hard hit', what might be the implications for the student's learning process?

The individual: multiple voices

It is difficult to be intelligent, creative, compassionate and sensitive if you are feeling misunderstood, frustrated, anxious, angry or disillusioned.

(Clarke 1983: 7)

One of the elements that has emerged from postmodernist thinking is recognition of the validity of multiple discourses (Lyons 1994). Not only does each discourse have value and deserve recognition, but postmodernism asserts that different discourses and reactions are present in each person experiencing different contexts. Further, Pedersen (1997) alludes to recent theoretical thinking that suggests that, inside each person, at least 'one thousand voices' speak messages from significant others, internalized since birth. All the 'culture teachers' are there. Work by both Bakhtin (1986, 1990) and Searle (1992) seems to support this view, acknowledging that all actions by humans are dialogically linked and all utterances within conversations necessarily relate to each other (in Shotter 1995).

These ideas have implications for the counsellor's task. What voice or voices does the counsellor listen to? What is real or unreal? Can the counsellor tolerate the anxiety, ambiguity and possible chaos of the presented cacophony of views, reflections, memories, desires etc.? These are the sort of issues that counsellors in training and in ongoing practice have to face.

Further, from the student's perspective, how does the context of higher education determine the student's behaviour, their thinking, feeling and sensing faculties, their sense of control and so on? They may have come from a setting in which they were perfectly comfortable and secure, whereas now they may experience considerable threats to self-esteem and self-confidence, leading to panic attacks, isolation, despair and depression, perhaps engaging in antisocial or deviant behaviour (e.g. vandalism, excessive drinking, drug-taking).

Mearns (1994) has written a very moving account of working with someone whose personality was broadly divided between a spirited young girl and a nun. Mearns contextualizes this work, not dramatically within the arena of multiple personality, but rather within a standard range of human psychology, in which a person may become caught between aspects of themselves. He assisted the client in working out these internal psychological tensions by attending conscientiously and accepting equally all expressed aspects, even when these dimensions were in direct contradiction. This case study by a person-centred therapist demonstrates the counsellor's role in facilitating the reintegration of separated aspects of the client's self, strengthening the student's sense of self and thus contributing to their capacity to engage in academic learning.

The ethnic identity models offered earlier in this chapter demonstrate particular stages where a person's self can be so invalidating of their internal experience that they capitulate to the dominant view and reject themselves.

The counsellor's work with individuals who conceive themselves to be 'different' or 'alternative' thus focuses on that individual's experiencing of the world. As that experiencing is articulated in multiple ways during the therapy, the varying attitudes (or internalized voices) may be heard by the clients themselves. Once spoken and heard by both counsellor and client, these different voices and tendencies can be psychologically reintegrated in consciousness, offering the client new opportunities for understanding and, hopefully, acceptance of their 'selves', however 'different' they may be. Indeed, Mearns describes this process as one of empathic mediation and likens it, in part, to working with couples in therapy, where one partner can hear the other partner afresh, precisely because of the therapist's presence and focus.

The crowd: skin as the point of contact with the world

We have focused on individual experiences of difference within the self and offered a highly compacted version of the counsellor's task, where broadly similar responses might be evoked from different theoretical perspectives (e.g. client-centred, psychodynamic, gestalt, TA, postmodernism). Issues of 'difference', however, can also reside in the perception of others. The more pernicious forms express themselves in the various 'isms' and phobias, e.g. racism, sexism, homophobia. In these circumstances the 'skin' is often the point of negative contact with the world. Defining 'skin' in its broader meaning – that which is visible to the perceiver – anyone with a skin complaint, disfigurement, disability, unusual mannerisms and behaviour, different dress style, different features, different skin colour and so on may be subjected to negative perceptions, judgements and acts from others of the other/dominant/majority group. Suddenly, the subject of these perceptions is cast in the role of 'differentness', as the outsider, the odd one.

Negative perceptions of others involve judgements that assume some form of superiority in the perceiver and communicate 'deficiency' to the perceived. Sustained exposure to such negative perceptions and actions can severely damage a person's sense of self-worth (Lago and Thompson 1996). Student victims of social ostracism, bullying and harassment may often turn to student counselling services feeling alienated from the world. In counselling, the experience of respect and acceptance counter the alienation they experience outside: to be accepted within this relationship means, crucially, that one is not totally alienated. Of course, the cumulative effect of the counsellor's work with such individuals will often amount to much more than this one aspect of offering acceptance and attention, but it does, in and of itself, deeply justify the humanizing and therapeutic effect upon the client.

Beyond this individualized role, the counsellor may also choose to work within the wider context, in this way contributing to the greater well-being of those within the university or college community (Lago and Shipton 1994). Such initiatives offer enormous potential for learning about selves, about others, about problem exploration, about human relating.

The three core aims of the work of university or college counsellors has long been defined by their professional association as:

- work with individuals;
- preventative work (e.g. study skills, orientation programmes, making friends, developing confidence, anxiety management);
- development work (e.g. listening skills, providing training for student organisations, staff development programmes, etc.).

However, both the authors of this chapter know of only a few examples where workshops or discussion groups have been held to explore issues such as bullying or racism. Particular circumstances – for example, where there has been a spate of harassing behaviour in halls of residence – may offer the possibility of ready-made group learning opportunities. Counsellors are sometimes invited in to assist in facilitating these potentially difficult scenarios. The student counsellor in these circumstances can be a potent catalyst in facilitating group learning thus contributing developmentally to students' social and emotional development. This work should not be taken on lightly, and counsellors should assess their own comfort, expertise and experience before embarking upon such ventures. Clinical supervision of any such groupwork is also strongly advised.

During recent years, policies have been drawn up to address situations of harassment (general, sexual, racial) and/or pejorative treatment, such as an AIDS sufferer being discriminated against, in the university or college setting. Counsellors have often been either the stimulus for such initiatives or key players in the committee work that has produced such policies.

A further aspect of the counsellor's wider role is that of contributing to staff development. Workshops and courses for staff inevitably focus on the enhancement of interpersonal skills, particularly in the staff–student relationship (see e.g. Lago and Shipton 1994). Examples will include courses like the following:

- counselling skills;
- personal tutoring;
- supervising postgraduates;
- dealing with student emergencies;
- groupwork;
- resident tutoring;
- supporting international students.

In all of these, excellent opportunities exist for discussion about and consideration of student differences in various organizational settings including lecture theatres, halls of residence, students' union facilities, laboratories, advice centres and so on. Discerning staff development units encourage all staff, be they academic, administrative, secretarial, technical or residential, to pursue their own training development. Within this domain the counsellor is able to contribute to a college structure where differences are respected and valued. However, there are difficulties and dilemmas involved, and some counsellors, by virtue of their personality preferences and/or theoretical orientation, might not find the challenge of working in a more public way, whether as a convenor, chair, trainer or facilitator, appropriate. Other problems experienced by the authors of this chapter include:

- groups who have been pressurized to attend, leading to resistance and negative effects on the aims and objectives of the course or workshop;
- working as a sole trainer or with a trainer who has been imposed upon you;
- facilitating a training group where participants (students and staff) are also your counselling clients and where there has not been an opportunity to prepare them for meeting you in another role.

Despite the complexities, ethical preoccupations and organizational challenges of engaging in these preventative and developmental tasks, in parallel with the task of individual counselling, the benefits can ripple out from those directly participating to others they are in association with. Positive examples that we have been involved with include supporting friendship groups of a student who had committed suicide, successfully intervening in the stuck and polarized group dynamics of an academic staff team, facilitating a case discussion involving colleagues holding different viewpoints, and training staff to work more sensitively with international students.

The above section demonstrates the importance of the counsellor's task in all three professional domains. Riding roughshod over the issues of difference are all the negative slurs of deficiency, otherness, negativity, 'non-humanness', etc. as well as the complete gamut of negative actions (bullying, harassment, racism, sexism, exclusion, etc.). By engaging with these issues on all three levels, the college counsellor, alongside other staff, has a unique opportunity to contribute to the wider social learning environment of higher education.

Issues of difference in students have the capacity to push a college's alarm bells! In understanding, tolerating and accepting difference the college counsellor has an enormous part to play in the healthy functioning of the organization.

Particular student groupings

Mature students

As has been noted, the numbers of mature students have grown considerably over the last twenty years. This growth has been particularly evident in pre-1992 universities, where in some cases the mature student population (those over 21) make up 60–75 per cent of the student community. In researching this chapter, one counselling service from a North London university stated that as over 75 per cent of their students were mature students, 'traditional students' often felt more isolated. This trend is likely to continue and intensify. Following the disappearance of the binary divide between polytechnics and universities in 1992, the Dearing report, with its hope of broadening higher education for underrepresented groups, is likely to herald a change in the binary divide between FE and HE, and between full-time and part-time education. A major growth area is likely to be those already in work, lone parents, adults previously alienated from education – in short, mature students.

Some years ago a male postgraduate student requested urgent counselling. He was a self-financing student in his early forties who, having been made redundant, chose to do a postgraduate course in an applied social science subject. Sadly, he began to experience very negative reactions and treatment from the rest of his course group. Much of the course methodology was based upon student presentation of seminars and group discussions, and he had engaged enthusiastically in the learning process. He was already somewhat experienced in this field and enjoyed relationships elsewhere with some eminent practitioners. The group, it appeared, had come to resent his eagerness, his knowledge, his apparent political biases (different to their own) and found ways of 'ousting' him, including ridicule, non-invitation to social events, pressurizing the tutorial staff to have him removed and so on. The group dynamics became so bad that the course tutor and the head of department were driven to have special interviews with him in which they encouraged his withdrawal from the course (even negotiating a fee remission to induce his resignation). It was at this point that the student, by now experiencing terrible anxiety and turmoil, turned to the Students' Union Advice Centre, the Counselling Service, the Harassment Network and the university regulations. Even so he found that little could be done to save the situation, and eventually he left. For a long time afterwards he suffered terrible flashbacks and mood swings, but fortunately, the counselling service concerned had maintained an openness to being contacted after he left, thus affording occasional opportunities up to a year later of psychologically processing this experience. He was eventually able to redirect his energies and commitment onto a more receptive programme.

In many counselling services mature students represent a sizeable proportion of the caseload, if not a majority. Counsellors often organize and attend induction meetings or fairs for mature students at the beginning of the academic year, and often are involved in the writing of handbooks and other information for them. But largely (and rightfully some would argue) mature students receive a similar service to other students, and many would prefer not to be singled out for special treatment. From a counselling point of view, however, there are often important differences to the work carried out. A mature student's reason for getting a qualification is often more complex than just finding employment. Many will see a course as a life-changing experience, in which they have made a huge psychological, emotional and financial investment. Many, of course, will view the qualification as a way of escaping poverty or benefits. There can also be difficulties in returning to formal education. Those who have attended Access courses are surprisingly among those most affected by the change, as they are moving from a student-centred environment to a subject-centred environment. Mature students may present for counselling doubtful and anxious about studies. The prospect of failure can be traumatic, especially if connections are made with other failures in their lives. Equally, personal issues with students over 30 tend to be more deep-seated, and help has often previously been sought with other agencies. This can mean that the student has more psychological resources to cope with difficult material; at the same time, it can lead them to have more reason to doubt their potential. Because of all this, the therapeutic work can be longer-term. Finally, financial difficulties can often compound personal issues and add to a sense of hopelessness. A referral to a financial adviser or a student union welfare adviser is often a crucial step in allowing the client to concentrate on the personal material within the counselling.

Generally, counselling services in the UK do not offer focused services to mature students. Elsewhere, such as in Australia and Canada, there are examples of specific services co-ordinated by counselling services for mature students. At the University of Western Sydney, Macarthur, the Mature Age Student Kollective (MASK), established by the counselling service, offers monthly events (skills, workshops, groups, etc.) and a register of mature age students which students can use to facilitate the formation of study groups. Fanshawe College in Ontario, Canada (an arts and technology college), has a mature student counsellor who dedicates her time solely to working with adult learners. This involves induction, counselling, advice and an extensive programme of seminars on subjects such as 'Overcoming procrastination', 'Discover your learning style', 'How is your family dealing with you as a student?'

Mark Phippen (1997), in his response as Chair of the Association for University and College Counsellors to the Dearing Report, outlined possible implications for counselling services. Among these was a need for counselling services to further consider the 'non-traditional student'. In relation to mature and part-time students, services need to consider extending the 9–5 counselling provision. Phippen states that mature students and other non-traditional students will need to have 52-week access to counselling services. He also questions how 'user-friendly' counselling services actually are. Beyond these suggestions, we contend that the preventative and developmental aspects of the counsellor's work could be extensively developed with particular groups of students. These and other issues certainly need to be addressed if, as is expected, the student community is broadened further.

International students

International students are a growing population in most universities. Because of the financial benefits they bring to an institution in a climate of financial retrenchment and cutback, they are likely to be of increasing importance in the future.

Various training manuals and videos have been produced for use in staff training programmes in relation to international students (Lago 1990; UKCOSA 1993a; UKCOSA 1993b; Green *et al.* 1994). Counsellors and international student advisers are in a unique position to tutor such courses, thus helping to sensitize the environment to international student needs.

Many institutions now have international student advisers offering information and guidance to international students. They are heavily used, yet relatively few international students (especially from the main recruiting countries, e.g. Hong Kong and Malaysia) use counselling services. This is not to say that international students do not experience emotional difficulty. On the contrary, many may suffer bereavement, family break-up and other difficulties on top of culture shock and quite acute feelings of isolation.

Okorocha (1994, 1997a, b) outlines possible reasons why international students may not use counselling. First, there is a stigma attached to counselling, which is often linked by international students to psychiatry.

There is also a sense that counselling goes against the cultural orientation of many students, who are more used to dealing with family members and elders when coping with emotional difficulties. Okorocha also found there was a misunderstanding of the process, many international students expecting counselling to offer advice and guidance. The Western-based emphasis of counselling on non-directiveness and self-help can lead an international student to leave a counselling interaction feeling let down. Some students in the survey also felt that counsellors had a lack of sensitivity to other cultures which made the experience seem monocultural and restricted the possibility of a working alliance being established.

To make clinical counselling with clients from overseas a safer and more respectful environment, Eleftheriadou (1996) advocates the taking of a 'psycho-racial biography' as a foundation. This would include a client's sense of their ethnic grouping, their understanding of their family's origins and how these impact upon them in their present circumstances, their belief system, their relationship to other groups in society, their own sense of who they are, what limits they experience in terms of friendship and partnership and so on. This helps to give the client's own cultural influences validity, and allows them to bring these to the counselling process, giving permission for these to coexist with the present cultural influences. She continues: 'If the counsellor is able to be multicultural, that is give enough space for another cultural view to be expressed during the relationship, the students will feel safe enough to explore their own and the new cultural context.'

Okorocha (1994) offers some possible thoughts about how to improve services offered to international students. These include cross-cultural training for counsellors and informal group sessions that replicate the international expectations of international students. These two aspects are presently being explored by Pedersen (1994) and a research team involving universities from Canada, Australia and the UK.

Pedersen has long been researching and developing the notion of a triad training model which pays particular attention to cultural difference. The basis of the approach is that the more culturally different the client is to the counsellor, the less chance the counsellor has of understanding the client's internal dialogue. The model is designed to make explicit the internal dialogue of the client in a simulated counselling session in which a counsellor trainee is present with a client, a coached pro-counsellor who feeds back the positive aspects of the interaction, and a coached anti-counsellor who feeds back the negative. The client and the pro- and anti-counsellors are ideally from a similar cultural background. The counsellor in the role-play hears not only the client's voice, but also the positive and negative voices of the colleagues occupying or playing out the alter-ego states of the pro- and anti-counsellors. Pedersen hopes that, 'As the counsellor becomes more familiar with the positive and negative messages that a culturally different client might be thinking but not saying, the counsellors will be able to incorporate those messages into the explicit counselling interview.' It is clear that this and other cross-cultural techniques need to be developed and assimilated into training for counsellors.

Humphrys (1997) at the University of Leeds and Barty at South Bank University have been piloting groups for international students that focus on acquiring cultural competencies that will help them become more used to the new academic and sociocultural environment. The courses are based on research being carried out by Westwood, Barker, Ishiyama and Mak (1994), who have developed programmes of training in sociocultural skills acquisition for newly arrived immigrants and international students. The programme takes the form of a six-week course, two hours per week, offered early in the student's academic career and focusing on particular skills such as interjection in lectures, clarification, social conversation and seeking help. The group enables students from various cultural backgrounds to compare their experience with the expectations of British culture and identify the differences. The students then have the opportunity to develop a 'cultural map', perhaps featuring a behaviour that is prevalent in British culture, but different to their own, and which can be explained and illustrated by the trainers and practised with support and positive criticism from the group. The group offers many possibilities for international students, such as a safe place to practise skills, a support group, knowledge that others are experiencing similar difficulties to them, attention from trainers who are sensitive to their experiences, and an entrée into the cultural environment in which they find themselves.

Students from ethnic minority groups

Various research studies quoted in the Dearing Report indicate that, relative to their share in the population, ethnic minorities overall are now better represented in higher education than whites. This general overrepresentation was similar at all age levels. However, despite this encouraging development, recognition has to be made of groups who continue to have low participation rates. Different research studies cite specifically Bangladeshis (and within this group Bangladeshi women), 'Black-other' and Black-Caribbeans, particularly Afro-Caribbean men (Modood and Shiner 1994, UCAS 1996, Ackland 1997).

Particular institutions (post-1992 universities) in London and the Midlands have differential concentrations of ethnic minority groups, this factor often reflecting large ethnic minority populations in the general vicinity (Modood 1993). Dearing also notes research showing that:

- these universities accept, on average, greater numbers of students with non-standard entry qualifications (Taylor 1992);
- black students, on average, are older than white students and those from the Indian sub-continent (Hogarth *et al.* 1997);
- there is some evidence that selection bias or racial discrimination has taken place in admissions to higher education (Taylor 1992; Modood and Shiner 1994).

Bell (1996) offers several case scenarios involving ethnic minority clients using student counselling services. She also discusses work by Sara Brown at the University of Hertfordshire, who noted (1994: 76) that about 11 per cent of clients attending the service came from minority ethnic groups, whereas 18 per cent of the total student population was comprised of students from such groups. In the Counselling Service Annual Report (1994) she postulates that black people experiencing distress may be more likely initially to use medical services. She suggests, and various reports indicate, that black people are more likely to be treated at the 'heavier end of the medical model approach to psychological problems, e.g. medication, E.C.T., locked ward, confinement etc.' (Skellington and Morris 1992).

Brown goes on to hypothesize other reasons for this apparent underrepresentation of minority ethnic groups in her counselling service statistics. Some preferred to use political methods to attend to issues of discrimination and racism, while others were deterred by the apparent 'newness' of the concept of counselling, and its concomitant (mis)under-standings by some minority groups who link it to specific issues only, like marriage, immigration or social welfare problems. Some students believed it was not possible for people outside their culture to understand their problems, while for some it would have been a shaming experience to discuss their problems outside the family.

Certainly, as regards this particular group of students, colleges in general and counselling services in particular need to consider very seriously the importance of the appointment of counsellors from a range of ethnic origins as well as of both genders. The importance of role-modelling cannot be underestimated here. These general pleas for staffing policies are generally accepted by student counsellors in Britain, who as a professional body are dedicated to equality of opportunity. However, limited resourcing often means that there is a scarcity of new posts to be filled.

Gender identity and sexual orientation as differences

> Successful and creative study requires students to commit themselves
> to the work and be comfortable with their aggression and sexuality.
>
> (Noonan 1986: 122)

The following scenarios are offered as a sample of issues that have been
presented to counsellors of students over recent years. None of these
scenarios are literal cases, but they are derived from cumulative experiences
of counselling in university settings over two decades.

A student had been consulting a counsellor for eighteen months,
more or less on a weekly basis, during term-time. Her presenting
problems were recurring bouts of depression combined with difficulties
in relationships. Various complex themes emerged over the months of
consultation, featuring a church-influenced background that was imbued
with guilt, an early history of immigration to the UK and particularly
painful experiences at school of tense relationships. As a way of coping,
she came to acknowledge that over the years she had developed very
sophisticated behaviours for keeping people at a distance – only very
few ever got to be trusted enough to come closer . . . but never too
close. Apart from a couple of very painful arranged dates that proved
excruciating, she had been unable to dare to embark on any relationships.

During the forty-fifth session the client tentatively handed the
counsellor a letter, requesting that it be read (silently): 'Dear . . . ', it
read, 'I fear that I am gay physically yet everything in my being screams
against that. . . . '

The counselling service was approached by a male, mature student in
his final year of a degree. The opening line of the first interview began:
'I've come to see you to see if you can help me deal with the
consequences, particularly institutionally, of having a gender identity
transfer operation . . . I hope when I return next year, as I am going to
withdraw this year on medical grounds, that I shall be a woman. . . . '

A local doctor had referred a postgraduate student to the counselling
service. The student had presented with many physical ailments over a
period of time and the doctor was very concerned. He had gleaned that
all was not well in the student's family, particularly in the extended

family. Despite various tests and appropriate examinations, no specific medical conditions were discovered or diagnosed. Nevertheless the student kept attending the surgery, eventually pleading with the doctor to have 'that operation that changed one's sexual identity'.

As such operations require, by medical convention and law, supportive reports from physicians and from a psychotherapist with whom the client has been working already for two years, the client's request for subsequent referral to the student counsellors was a source of great relief for the doctor, who could not see a way through this very complicated set of life circumstances and symptoms.

The counsellor worked with the client for many months. In the client's perceived reality, a gender transfer operation would achieve an outcome that seemed to remove all family pressures from him, thus releasing him into an anxiety-free state. However, the essential fact that he did not have, nor had ever had, feelings, intuitions or sensations that informed him he was in the 'wrong body' (the very issue that is explored in great detail in the compulsory psychotherapy phase described above) substantially mitigated against his case to have the operation. The counsellor, who continued to work with the client for several more months, had to withstand a continuous pressurizing barrage of pleas to give the client permission to have the operation.

Jack was a racing cyclist who also took part in road-running each winter. He was a very healthy-looking, tanned young man. His whole family were similarly very active, father and son often competing in the same races. Jack had not made many friends at university, despite nearing the end of his second year. Like many clients, he was extremely anxious about what judgements the counsellor might impose on his difficulties. The first few counselling sessions were spent looking at various dimensions of his family relationships. On the fifth session, and obviously under great personal strain, he struggled to tell the counsellor that he enjoyed cross-dressing and he had found a place in Soho where . . .

The enormous personal pain and discomfort experienced by these clients makes one wonder how they were able to keep studying successfully. Ellen Noonan's quote, used above to introduce this section, becomes absolutely relevant in these stories. To manage their studies and the other 'normal' pressures students experience, and then on top to deal with these issues, leaves one deeply respectful of their strength in adversity.

Issues of change in counselling services

Various commentators have noted the increased severity of problems presented by students to university and college counselling services. Sadly, the onset of a mental illness can often occur in late adolescence, which may result in neurotic symptoms (anxiety states, phobias, depressions, obsessions and compulsions) or psychotic episodes (psychosis, schizophrenia, manic depression). In these particular examples of sometimes very serious mental ill health, the student's behaviour will eventually mark them out as different. Counsellors are often amongst the first in the organization to be contacted concerning a student's 'strange' or bizarre behaviour. In the most extreme of cases, doctors, psychiatric social workers and psychiatrists may all become involved in the treatment process. Such examples often create great distress to those friends, relations and staff members who are in close relation to the ill student and counsellors sometimes end up also supporting these 'carers'.

The increased incidence of these dramatic, acute, crisis events, which have the capacity to upset a wide circle of others, begs serious questions, not only of counselling services and their levels of resource and competence, but also of the role of higher education as an extension of community psychiatric care. Students who have reasonably recovered from periods of mental ill health have every right to enrol at universities and be appropriately supported while they learn. However, the demands imposed by increased numbers of students presenting with very critical psychiatric concerns are becoming quite excessive, especially in these times of reduced psychiatric resources.

Given the above circumstances, counsellors are faced with the difficult question: should they contribute to the development of universities as therapeutic communities and focus their work on those who are clinically very distressed or offer a reduced contact to a wider range of generally distressed students that present to them? What is clear, however, is that a very complex interplay features between the individual, familial and cultural perspectives of students' lives. The challenges to student counsellors, in terms of their knowledge base, their clinical practice, their intervention strategies in the college organization, etc., become increasingly formidable in the present context of enlarged student populations, movements towards less personal contact between tutors and students in the educational methods employed, and the rapid increase of usage of computer communications and information (Lago 1996). How counsellors are going to handle these and other rapidly changing elements in the higher education environment, while maintaining their valuing of individuals (students and staff), is going to prove an interesting and challenging process with very few easy guidelines or precedents to follow.

Final thoughts

The student body is now much more diverse than it was thirty years ago. The notion of the 'traditional student' (age 18–21 from a middle-class family) is fast disappearing. The education system itself is changing fast. With the likely increase of distance learning, the massive impact of IT on traditional teaching methods and the launch of the virtual university, boundaries are being moved in the educational environment all the time. The bewildering nature of these developments, however, indicates that the role of counselling is likely to expand. In a recent briefing paper for the DFEE entitled 'Supporting learner autonomy' (McNair 1997), McNair emphasizes and discusses the importance of 'guidance'. In the context of this paper, guidance is the catch-all term to describe advice, tutoring, careers guidance and counselling. McNair explains that, for students to meet the challenge of a changing, less secure educational and employ-ment environment, they will need access to appropriate guidance and counselling. He goes on to say that:

> The changes of the last decade have already placed our system for meeting these needs under great pressure, but the future is likely to bring more change, not less. Expansion in some form is likely to continue and with it a continuing diversification of students, demanding more individualised responses, precisely as institutions struggle to cope with larger numbers. The lack of common cultural assumptions about the nature and purposes of HE will call for better induction, while a shift towards funding through the learner rather than the institution will force institutions to become more sensitive to the needs of individuals who will be more like clients and less like beneficiaries!

This statement has enormous implications for counselling services and how they respond to difference. As students start to pay fees for their education, they will become more demanding and expect more in forms of support and guidance. They will also expect, and institutions will want to provide, 'individualized responses' to student need. These changes will encourage services to treat clients less like a homogeneous group and more like groups to be targeted. It is also likely that counselling service work on the preventative and developmental side is likely to be on a par with individual counselling work. Mature students will require support groups and seminar programmes; international students are likely to want support in line with their cultural expectations and actual needs; and ethnic minority students will want counselling teams that reflect the diversity of the student community.

All of this, of course, has resource implications. As many colleagues who are struggling with waiting lists will know, taking on new substantial activities will have an effect on the resources for coping with the massive demands of one-to-one work. However, the new environment perhaps demands a new approach and maybe a change in priorities for services.

Counsellors may have to become more vigorous and involved in the feedback process and policy development mechanisms of their organizations. In addition to working with individual clients and training groups, they may have to engage in the wider debates and decision-making processes, seeking to influence the educational endeavour in ways which will prove conducive to an increasingly diverse student population.

Counselling services in Australia, Canada and the USA have already broadened the way they work, and counselling is often one of many services on offer to students. This broadening out, however, cannot be achieved without requisite changes in funding. However, this is also a time of opportunity for counselling services in the UK. After Dearing, the issue of 'guidance' is being discussed in every university and college in the UK. It is important that counselling services present their views about the diversification of the student body and changes in the learning environment alongside tutors, careers staff and those offering welfare support and advice within the institution.

What is clear is that 'difference' is going to be a crucial issue in the immediate future, as a dynamic in our clinical work and the way we plan our services.

Bibliography

Ackland, T. (1997) paper from a seminar on widening participation in higher education, 27 March.

Atkinson, D., Morten, G. and Sue, G.W. (1989) *Counselling American Minorities: A Cross Cultural Perspective*, Dubuque, IA: William C. Brown.

Bakhtin, M. (1986) *Speech Genres and Other Late Essays*, trans. W. Mcgee, Austin: University of Texas Press.

Bakhtin, M. (1990) *Art and Answerability: Early Philosophical Essays*, trans. M. Holquist and V. Liapuncy, Austin: University of Texas Press.

Barty, A. (1988) 'Social cultural competencies for success', unpublished research paper, South Bank University.

Bell, E. (1996) *Counselling in Further and Higher Education*, Milton Keynes: Open University Press.

Brown, S. (1994) *Counselling Service Annual Report*, Hatfield: University of Hertfordshire.

Clarke, P. (1983) 'The work of a student counsellor', a University of Sheffield working party paper quoted in the annual report of the University Counselling Service, 1991–2.

Eleftheriadou, Z. (1996) 'Notions of culture', in S. Sharples (ed.), *Changing Cultures: Developments in Cross Cultural Theory and Practice*, London: UKCOSA.

Fanshawe College: http:// www. fanshawe.on.ca/services/studentlife/maststgp.htm.

Green, D., Holliday, J. and Lago, C.O. (1994) *They Look at Your Face and See a Flag*, staff training video, University of Sheffield Television Service.

Helms, J.E. (1984) 'Towards a theoretical model of the effects of race on counselling: a black and white model', *The Counselling Psychologist*, 12: 153–65.

Hogarth, T., Macguire, M., Pitcher, J., Purcell, K. and Wilson, R. (1997) 'The participation of non-traditional students in higher education', Warwick: University of Warwick Institute for Employment Research.

Humphrys, N. (1997) 'Report on social cultural competence programme', unpublished research paper, University of Leeds.

Lago, C.O. (1990) *Working with Overseas Students: A Staff Development Training Manual*, Huddersfield: British Council and University of Huddersfield.

—— (1996) 'Computer therapeutics: a new challenge for counsellors and psychotherapists', *Counselling*, 17(4), November.

Lago, C.O. and Shipton, G. (1994) *On Listening and Learning: Student Counselling in Further and Higher Education*, London: Central Book Publishing.

Lago, C.O. and Thompson, J. (1996) 'The triangle with curved sides: race and culture in counselling supervision', in G.A. Shipton (ed.), *The Art of Supervision*: Milton Keynes: Open University Press.

Lyons, D. (1994) *Postmodernity*, Buckingham: Open University Press.

McNair, S. (1997) *Getting the Most out of HE: Supporting Learner Autonomy*, Department for Education and Employment briefing paper.

Mature Age Student Kollective (MASK): http://www.macarthur.nws.edu.au/ssd/counselling/mask.htm.

Mearns, D. (1994) *Developing Person-centred Counselling*, London: Sage.

Modood, T. (1993) 'The number of ethnic minority students in British higher education: some grounds for optimism', *Oxford Review of Education*, 19(2): 167–82.

Modood, T. and Shiner, M. (1994) 'Ethnic minorities in higher education: why are there differential rates of entry?' London: Policy Studies Institute / WAS.

National Committee of Inquiry into Higher Education: Chairman Sir Ron Dearing (1997), *Higher Education in the Learning Society*, London: HMSO.

Noonan, E. (1986) 'The impact of the institution on psychotherapy', *Psychoanalytic Psychotherapy*, 2(2): 121–30.

Okorocha, E. (1994) 'Barriers to effective counselling of overseas students: implications for cross-cultural counselling', Society for Research into Higher Education 1994 conference, York.

—— (1997a) 'Cultural clues to student guidance', Association for Student Counselling Newsletter, February.

—— (1997b) 'Counselling international students: challenges and strategies', *Race and Cultural Education in Counselling (RACE) Journal*, 12, January.

Pedersen, P. (1994) 'Simulating the client's internal dialogue as a counsellor training technique', *Simulation and Gaming*, 25(1), March: 40–50, Sage Publications.

—— (1997) 'Workbook: hearing the self talk of culturally different clients', paper given at UKCOSA conference, 16 October, London.

Phippen, M. (1997) 'Implications for AUCC members of the Dearing Report', letter to AUCC executive (6 October).

Searle, J.R. *et al.* (1992) *(On) Searle on Conversation*, compiled and introduced by H. Parret and J. Verschuren, Amsterdam and Philadelphia: John Benjamins.

Shotter J. (1995) 'In conversation: joint action, shared intentionality and ethics', *Theory and Psychology*, 5(1): 49–73.

Skellington, R. and Morris, P. (1992) *Race in Britain Today*, London: Sage and Open University Press.

Taylor, P. (1992) 'Ethnic group data and applications to higher education', *Higher Education Quarterly*, 46(4): 359–73.

UCAS (1996) *Qualified Applicants: 'Those Who Did Not Enter Higher Education'*, statistical survey, Cheltenham: UCAS.

UKCOSA (1993a) *The UKCOSA Manual*, London: UKCOSA.

UKCOSA (1993b) *Partners in Discovery: Developing Cultural Awareness and Sensitivity*, a training video and trainers' guide, UKCOSA.

Westwood, M.J., Barker, M., Ishiyana, F.L. and Mak, A.S. (1994) 'Developing role-based social competencies: a model of inter-cultural training for immigrants', *Journal of Career Development*, 20: 50–63.

9 No client (and no counsellor) is an island

Attending to the culture of the educational setting

Eileen Smith

Introduction

In this chapter I will argue, paraphrasing Donne, that no client (and no counsellor) is 'an island, entire of itself'; both are 'part of the continent, part of the main'. I will suggest that counsellors in education will have more to offer if they struggle to be conscious of and reflect on the culture in which they work and of which they are part. I will draw here on clinical, training and consultative work to consider how counsellors might think about their experience in relation to prevailing social and cultural forces in their institutions, their clients and, not least, themselves.

Culture is of course a broad term, described by Raymond Williams as 'one of the two or three most complicated words in the English language' (1976: 76). The discipline of cultural studies provides some clarification of the sense in which I will use the term. Hartley begins his definition: 'The social production and reproduction of sense, meaning and consciousness' (Hartley *et al.* 1994: 68). Hall (1997) writes of how culture was used in the 1960s to describe 'attitudes, values, ways of life, forms of relationships, the structures of meaning that people use to interpret what's going on in their lives'. In earlier writing he argues that culture may encompass sets of assumptions, a common sense which we never question and which may come to operate unconsciously:

> Common sense shapes our ordinary, practical, everyday calculations and appears as natural as the air we breathe. It is simply 'taken for granted' in practice and thought, and forms the starting-point (never examined or questioned) from which every conversation begins . . .
>
> (1988: 8)

I would suggest that counsellors in education should pay heed to the common sense and complexities of their contexts and their own feelings in them. When we work with individuals we may begin with what is currently troubling the client, perhaps take a history, find out about family relationships, form an impression based on our own experience and feelings about being with the client and then reflect on the possible meanings of all this material. With our institutions too we need to know the current issues, history and background, to monitor our feelings and ponder on the meanings for ourselves and other members. McCaughan and Palmer argue that 'Human beings are constituted as *persons* by the network of relations and transactions of which they are a part' (1994: 98), while Armstrong (1991) contends that 'emotional experience is very rarely located within a purely individual space'. Many counsellors will accept such views fairly readily in terms of thinking of clients' development or transference and counter-transference issues but find it more difficult to think about the interrelatedness of social and cultural forces and the process of counselling.

Many who work one-to-one have little interest in systems. They tend to emphasize the individual, to look for explanations of difficulty in personal histories, immediate relationships or, at best, group dynamics; in so doing they may underemphasize the impact of the context on clients, teams and themselves and their own involvement in creating and sustaining an emotional culture. I would contend that, in order to work well in an educational context, counsellors need more than an understanding of adolescent development, learning processes and the therapeutic relationship. Each client and each counsellor is unique but they are also part of a system which they influence and which influences them. Counsellors therefore need to be aware of both the particular culture of their individual institution and of general social trends. Such reflection does not of course substitute for detailed attention to client material but it may supplement it. The awareness I suggest is partly a matter of conscious thinking about the effect of changes in local or national institutional structures and policies on the student body; another part of this approach is more subtle and calls for a questioning of what seems normal, everyday; yet another aspect calls for a capacity to make use of one's own feelings to make sense of and gain a fresh perspective on a shared culture.

I am aware of a number of influences which have led me to advocate such an interpretation of the task of a counselling service in an educational setting. My own counselling training included exploration of institutional issues and space for reflection on the course itself as a learning organization (Noonan and Spurling 1992). Having worked as a teacher and counsellor in different sectors of education I have been very struck by the range of meaning systems I have encountered in different schools, further education colleges, old and new universities. For several years now I have had a management role which has necessitated working on the boundary between different parts of my organization and their very distinct cultures and of the consequent struggle to be coherent in different discourses. Membership of a course on consultation and organizational processes and of group relations conferences has helped me think about the relatedness of different parts of an organization, the ubiquity of projection, the place of unconscious processes in working groups and the importance of grasping the significance of role and authority. I have benefited from visits of external consultants to work with my team, discussion with colleagues inside and outside my university and the thoughtfulness of supervisors who have been willing to address both the clinical and organizational aspects of my work. I have found both psychoanalytic and systems theory helpful; here I will draw particularly on concepts of containment, the organization-in-the-mind, social defences against anxiety and basic assumption functioning.

The prevailing emotional climate

Working with clients in a college of further education

I shall begin with some client work. My first paid counselling job was in a further education college in East London. I had lived in London for a few years and was quite familiar with inner city areas but was none the less struck by the poverty and deprivation in the part of London where the college was based. Many of the staff were young, keen and enthusiastic and wanted to make up to the young people and older Access students who used the college for the deprivations of their environment. This was before the ILEA was disbanded and there was considerable awareness of social injustice and a belief that education could help counteract this. In fact, a counselling service seminar entitled 'Why choose failure?' which aimed to explore emotional barriers to learning and development was met with a predominantly hostile response, as if the idea that students might make a contribution, however small, to their lack of success was an insulting attack and a denial of their structural disadvantage. Many of the staff used to compare the college with the school system – they stressed how unlike school teachers they were in that they attempted to respect the young people whom they taught and treat them as adults with the right to make their own decisions.

Over a period of time, I became aware of how students seemed to drift away from the college. Classrooms later in the year were often half empty and there were a number of students who, to my consternation, used to drift in and out of counselling and seemed surprised if I wrote to them after a missed session. I began to wonder if these students' needs for care were being ignored, if treating them as adults was actually a way of colluding with adolescent irresponsibility. I thought that students may have felt that no one noticed whether they were present or not and might actually have experienced some follow-up as a sign of concern rather than an intrusion on their independence. I was fresh from my counselling course and training placements in traditional universities and taken aback by the lack of perseverance and commitment I encountered.

This context was the background to counselling work with a young man in his early thirties. His life until this point had been spent drifting. The death of his mother and difficulty in relating to the rest of his family had led him to leave home very early; he had never settled, nor sustained any commitments to relationships or work. I felt he could have drifted out of college and out of counselling too but I made a point of taking a firm hold of him and following up any missed appointments. He could be very dismissive of his own experience but I insisted on taking it seriously. His course replicated his family history in a particularly difficult way. He was the fourth boy in a family of five. The next child had been a girl and he had always felt a mistake, not wanted, that his parents had been waiting for this girl who was given much more attention and importance than he was. His course was being reorganized and his year's work was considerably disrupted by the staff taking time off to plan for the following year. To add insult to injury, extra resources were allocated to provide for the coming year and he was full of anger about this. We worked weekly for eighteen months exploring the feelings of rage and rejection which made him want to disparage himself, me and our work together and so sabotage the painful hope of development. He did complete the course and was accepted on to a more advanced course in another institution. One can never be sure, but I suspect that without the counselling intervention he might easily have dropped out of college; a premature departure might have further fuelled his sense of failure.

Another student's difficulties also demonstrated a need for stability and attachment. A young Bangladeshi in his late teens, he was referred by a tutor concerned about his over-interest in her and apparent inability to make normal friendships with other students. The student, who seemed a boy rather than a young man to me, began to write his teacher love letters. I felt he was desperately trying to attach to something or someone. When I asked about his family he described a father who was a very important person in his community. It was difficult to get any picture of his mother. He became more disturbed, having very bad panic attacks and imagining the college computers were speaking directly to him. When he came to relate that his parents were going back to Bangladesh, leaving him alone with his younger brother in London, I became worried enough to move out of my formal counselling role and invite his parents into college. His father came and it was clear that he was not the grand man of the student's imagination but someone who was unemployed and had never quite found a place in his new country. The client's problems in some ways reflected the rather precarious situation of his community. The work with him was less successful; despite my attempts to understand his internal world and the influence of his social context he became more disturbed and was admitted to hospital for a while.

I had some difficulty in finding a way to work in this culture; I had much to learn from and about it. At first I felt very puzzled and inadequate and struggled not to be overwhelmed but to keep a helpful distance which would enable me to think, to find a balance between the values I brought with me from my counselling training and a necessary adaptation and response to the setting. With the students I have described and many more an important part of the work was to be reliable and containing (i.e. being able to take in, bear and reflect on their experience); in so doing I aimed to counter-balance aspects of the culture prevailing in the college. My thinking about the culture informed my practice: I worked with clients' transference to the institution as well as to me and aimed to help them become more connected by suggesting links between their various roles as students, family members and counselling clients.

Training in a new university

I moved from this further education college to work in a polytechnic which became a new university. I have described elsewhere (Smith 1997a) the impact of the institution's change in status and rapid expansion on the work of the counselling service. All staff and students were affected. Increases in student numbers were not matched by increases in staffing; as a result teaching methods changed considerably and the opportunity for individual contact time with students was reduced.

Recently I offered academic staff a ten-week course in pastoral care; this took a morning a week and was split into two parts. In the first there was input by either myself or invited lecturers, and in the second, course members brought examples of their own work to discuss with the group. I enjoyed the work and I think my teaching was competent. I was, however, taken aback by the very positive feedback from course members and by the aspects of the course they reported liking best. Again and again they stressed how much they appreciated the small group work, the time to reflect and the opportunity to discuss their experience with colleagues.

I asked myself what I had done to elicit such a positive response, as I thought what I had provided was unexceptional in that it was obviously needed. I always got to the (very cold) room we had been allocated early, and set about arranging the chairs. I fussed to make sure that we had plentiful supplies of coffee. I was clear about the topics I could offer and then negotiated a detailed programme very carefully with members and checked my suggestions with them before finalizing the programme. I asked that everyone bring at least one issue to the second part of the group to discuss. I provided advance readings every week and sent them to people who had to miss a session. I tried to brief the visiting speakers carefully so that they understood something of the nature of the group. I shared some of my experience of working in the university with the academics and drew on my teaching background to make sure no one person was allowed to dominate discussion. I did listen to them and respect them and kept them in mind in between sessions. In short, I aimed to provide what good enough teachers and good enough counsellors I take it do provide. But clearly, such provision could no longer be taken for granted, could no longer be thought of as just what any decent course would deliver.

A colleague described similar feedback from the student members of the peer support training she runs. The most repeated remark about her is, 'You listen to us'. Counsellors reading this may think, 'Well of course – it's the basic counselling skill', yet clearly these students felt the need to comment, did not take it for granted that their experience would be taken seriously.

The surprise expressed in the remarks on these courses indicates something of the prevailing culture in the university to which these staff and students belong and points again to the necessary containing function of counselling and the need for counsellors to value what they can offer. I would link the surprise with the experience I sometimes got from counselling students in this setting, that they are very grateful for what I think of as very little. They return for a second session claiming to feel much better when I am still struggling to find some helpful formulation, having just begun to get a picture of their predicament. It does seem that the very fact of being listened to carefully is unusual and in itself often enables them to continue functioning; some, however, may be scared off by the 'being taken seriously' that counselling involves. In a discussion with a colleague about why some students who do not return after only one or two sessions leave the counsellor feeling dumped upon, we began to wonder if what was projected and left was their taking themselves seriously; after disburdening themselves they could retreat into their apparently coping selves. While this is disappointing, and while I would wish more students might take up the offer of ongoing work, I now think that the fact of the presence of a counselling service on campus to which students and staff can turn and return in itself represents an important validating of personal experience and fulfils a holding function.

Using our experience as members of the organization

I do not, however, want to imply that a counselling service is an oasis of stability, reflection, good sense, insight and benevolence, a retreat from the harsh world of the rest of the institution. It would be worrying if counsellors were insulated from the anxieties of those they work with. Moylan (1994) describes the dangers of contagion when working with people in distress but also demonstrates the opportunities for development in becoming aware of the pressures arising from unconscious defences against pain and the element of communication in the processes of projective identification. I have written elsewhere (Smith 1997b) about the tensions and projections that may be experienced within counselling teams operating in a climate dominated by anxieties about survival. Bell (1997) writes of counsellors in higher education mirroring the competition and rivalry of their student clients while Obholzer suggests that 'From an unconscious point of view, the education system is supposed to shield us from the risk of going under' (1994: 171–2). My understanding of how individual experience can be ignored in periods of institutional upheaval, and consequent planning of courses for staff and students to counter that tendency, was much heightened by a previous experience of a consultation to my service by David Armstrong, when loss of identity emerged as a strong theme.

The consultation took place at a time when the move to university status was very recent and expansion was at its height. All staff were under strain from these changes. The consultant began by asking each of us to draw without words a picture of the department in the context of the university with ourselves in it. My own drawing showed me, rather beleaguered, in a corner of my office surrounded by demanding colleagues, while up the stairs to the service came a long train of students seeking counselling. We talked about our pictures with one another and then:

> It came to the turn of a very experienced and long standing member of the department who worked on a part-time basis to present his picture. He then said with feeling that he had found himself quite unable to find and draw any image. All he had come up with was a list of single words. A little later he linked his inability to an experience of feeling, as he put it, 'de-centred as a person'. He said that he associated this experience with feeling that he was not acknowledged as a person by the University but only as a hired hand. This in turn reflected a number of recent changes and negotiations in respect of his contract.
> (Armstrong 1996)

Such a sense of being on the outside, of not belonging, is not unusual in members of counselling services, and may be one response to contact with clients' feelings of fragmentation. Armstrong, however, understood it not just in terms of the individual member's personal experience or as a mirroring of adolescent processes, but as a key to understanding something important about the university culture at a particular moment in time:

> Viewed from an organisational perspective, as a kind of organisational analogue, the Counsellor's personal experience represented, contained and gave expression to a broader dynamic. This dynamic could be seen as one in which the new University's preoccupation in a rather harsh competitive culture with raising student numbers, becoming more market oriented and cost effective, was leading implicitly to a construction of students (and by extension, of staff) not as members of the institution or the College community relating as whole persons to the whole body of the institution and its corporate life, but more as contractees, the means through which the institution made its living, the emotional equivalent of the hired hand.
>
> (Armstrong 1996)

Armstrong comments:

> What had begun as an expression of one individual's dis-ease with his own relation to the institution, could, now, be reframed and given new meaning as a representation or registration within the individual of a more pervasive experience of dis-ease within the whole institution. This 'dis-ease' . . . I would see as a factor in the state of mind that was the organisation there and then. From this vertex the counsellor's 'no-picture' and its accompanying emotional aura was, one might say, an offering to his colleagues which through his image of de-centredness, paradoxically re-centred all their experience.
>
> (Armstrong 1996)

I have quoted from this paper at length; it provides a clear illustration of the use of the concept of the organization-in-the-mind where the experiences of a person in role within a system are used to illuminate aspects of ' the emotional experience that is contained within the inner psychic space of the organisation and the interactions of its members' (Armstrong 1991). Most counsellors would be used to examining their own feelings in a session to see what might be learned about the client and the kind of relationship being established, but this example demonstrates how the exploration of apparently individual feeling may illuminate a shared social space and vice versa. The elucidation of my colleague's experience helped me put in a broader context the disengagement I sometimes encounter in students and my sense of being deskilled in response. The consultation brought a different perspective to my experience of students, immediate colleagues and other university staff and released some energy for re-engaging with the concerns it raised. Of course such insight is not won once and for always. Just as counsellors must encounter afresh with each new young client the force of adolescent drives, so they need constantly to rediscover and re-engage with the relatedness between the complexities of individual experience and current organizational processes.

Finding an identity in transition

A consultation to staff in a new university

During the academic year of David Armstrong's consultation to us I had the opportunity to work for eight meetings with a group of colleagues, clinical radiography lecturers, who were also trying to make sense of their experience and role as members of the university. Their struggle to work through a difficult transition and establish an appropriate professional identity in changed circumstances may illuminate issues of general concern for students and other staff.

In our first meetings the lecturers spoke of isolation and lack of identity. The post of Clinical Lecturer in Radiography had been created within the university only eighteen months before the consultation. Some of the group described being made redundant by the NHS before being re-employed by the university and the shock of that process. They were all faced with making a change from practice to teaching and/or of employer and prevailing culture. Their difficulty in being clear about their new roles was exacerbated by the fact that most had three different workplaces – two hospitals and the university. More than once they told me of how the hospitals failed to provide name badges (an important confirmation of legitimacy and identity) for their students. They described having no space in the university, insufficient secretarial back-up and technical support. They felt that communication with the university – experienced as outside themselves – was poor; there were 'a lot of meetings but no action'. They seemed to feel rather unsure of their professional standing, in awe of and rivalrous with their academic counterparts. In different ways they reiterated the same themes; they felt no one took time to consider their needs and that they had no real home or clear professional identity. The dislocation they described echoed in many ways the decentredness which became apparent in the consultation with the counselling team. The lecturers' preoccupations were similar to those of students who, whatever their subject, have to manage a role transition and establish an identity, tasks made more difficult if the institution does not recognize and support them.

The lecturers' needs for care and thoughtful attention during this transition were projected into their students, whom they sometimes described as if they were patients rather than students: most gave students their home telephone numbers and had no objection to being rung up late at night; they felt very guilty if students failed to learn. Their reluctance to relinquish a straightforward caring clinical role and anxiety about what was expected in their new teaching role led them, I thought, to be overprotective of their students. At the same time they were holding onto important values they brought from their previous professional experience. Many academic staff have been faced with similar adjustments in recent years as more and more emphasis has been placed on research and income generation with consequent reductions in the time and energy available for teaching and pastoral care. Like the radiography lecturers, and indeed like students, they are faced with a struggle to sustain a previous view of their world and corresponding sense of meaning while remaining open to, and striving to integrate, a new set of priorities.

All students have some need to depend on their environment and their lecturers. Because the work of radiographers, like that of any other caring profession, calls particular attention to dependency needs, their presence in the university highlights issues which may be uncomfortable for an institution preoccupied with activity and change. They remind us of vulnerability and the need for continuing care. Hoggett (1998) has argued that a culture which celebrates continual change wants to deny the inevitability of some dependence on others and the environment, and has little tolerance for chronicity. In fact, as the consultation proceeded, the anxieties associated with the nature of the clinical work became more apparent. There was discussion about the responsibility that was sometimes given inappropriately to their students because of NHS staff shortages; what would happen if a patient had a cardiac arrest while being escorted back to the ward by a student? In one meeting a group member produced a skull from his briefcase as if to remind us that their profession involved them in life and death issues. There were stories of doctors who made mistakes, of the use of potentially dangerous but cheaper dyes during some procedures, of disrespect for patients and of one student's distress at finding that much of radiotherapy was purely palliative. The insistent repetition of such concerns was partly due to a perception that they might be ignored in the new university setting where providing for dependency needs implied financial as well as emotional commitment. The lecturers and their students needed to tolerate and process many painful realities. In working with them I needed not only to acknowledge and respond to their personal distress but also to draw on my understanding of the system to which we all belonged and the forces active within it.

Identity and change in the wider society

Questions of identity and change are not of course confined to the two institutions I have concentrated on so far; they are prevalent in contemporary culture. It is beyond the scope of this chapter to enter into lengthy cultural analysis but I will indicate some areas of tension which may currently be influencing counselling work in educational settings. The issues themselves will change with time but the need to take account of the wider social context is ongoing.

At the time of writing the fields of both education and counselling are involved in hegemonic struggles. British universities and colleges went through a period of expansion and shift in ethos under the last Conservative government, and all sectors of education are still the focus of intense debate and government activity. Major inquiries chaired by Kennedy and Dearing have reviewed further and higher education; their reports (both 1997) have recommended far-reaching changes, including measures to widen participation in post-school provision. Some institutions are faced with anxieties about their ability to survive and many are seeking to clarify their role and purpose. Universities are in a state of flux, caught in the middle of a shift from elite to mass education; the competing demands of business, research, teaching and social justice contest for ideological and financial advantage. Moreover there is considerable uncertainty about the future in many universities. The implications of changes in student funding are as yet unclear; we may see more part-time students very conscious of their status as consumers. Shifts in the global economy may have serious repercussions on current and prospective international students and consequently on university budgets. Counsellors need to be aware of the possible effects of such conflicts and insecurities in their clients, colleagues and themselves.

Counsellors have particular issues about their own professional identity to manage at present. Coverage of counselling in the media is very mixed; there is considerable exposure but also a good deal of scepticism. Approving reports of teams of counsellors being called in to help victims of a disaster or shocking crime are matched by accounts of charlatans or naive do-gooders making unsubstantiated claims for the efficacy of counselling. Internally the field is fraught with issues of legitimacy – evidenced partly by the amount of energy being spent on NVQs, issues of accreditation and registration and comparisons with psychotherapy. Within educational establishments counsellors frequently meet with repeated requests to make the case for counselling provision, to justify expenditure on their services despite the increasing number of students seeking their help. The Dearing report made no explicit reference to counselling, an omission which could reduce confidence in those offering or using services. The relative paucity of respectable evaluation and research studies in counselling does not help the search for professional credibility, although daily work with clients may reinforce practitioners' conviction of their usefulness. Experience of such contradictions is common – and unsettling.

The extent and speed of change in education and the continuing conflict over meaning and purpose in the fields of both education and counselling are likely to continue for some time and perhaps merely reflect wider social trends. Hall (1992) discusses theories of identity in our period of late-modernity:

> the argument is that the old identities which stabilised the social world for so long are in decline, giving rise to new identities and fragmenting the modern individual as a unified subject. This so-called 'crisis of identity' is seen as part of a wider process of change which is dislocating the central structures and processes of modern societies and undermining the frameworks which gave individuals stable anchorage in the social world.
>
> (Hall *et al.* 1992: 274)

The theories he describes suggest that open, fragmented, contradictory selves and constant change are the norm for our times. Such a culture makes it difficult for everyone but perhaps especially for young people to manage change and establish at least working identities for themselves.

Thoughtful consideration of their specific difficulties may be found, *inter alia*, in Heyno (1997) and White (1997), who offer ways of linking cultural understanding with clinical experience in an educational context. They discuss the contribution of social forces to student disturbance; the former writes of the many contributing factors to suicides in universities and the reasons for institutions' reluctance to examine these openly; the latter explores the growth of 'normotic' illness in students in a market culture.

Basic assumption mentality

The appearance of basic assumption activity is not surprising in a culture as unsettled as ours. Bion (1961) introduced the notion of basic assumption mentality which, he suggests, operates unconsciously in groups when members' attempts to evade pain, conflict and anxiety lead them to avoid working with reality. Bion spoke of three basic assumptions, of pairing, fight-flight and dependency; these have been explored extensively in writing drawing on the group relations tradition (Colman and Geller 1985; Lawrence *et al.* 1996). Turquet suggested a fourth basic assumption – of one-ness (baO), where 'members seek to join in a powerful union with an omnipotent force, unobtainedly high, to surrender self for passive participation, and thereby to feel existence, well-being and wholeness' (1974: 76) .

I have noticed a tendency towards baO activity in some staff and student groups facing uncertainty, who take refuge from difference and difficulty by declaring an unreal group cohesion and set of values which brook no questioning. I encountered it recently with a group of 'nightliners' (students who offer a telephone listening service to other students). Although I had been invited to speak about the personal stress such an activity could arouse, it was very hard to promote any such exploration. Group members insisted on the friendship, solidarity and support in the group which seemed to offer identity and social life as well as an opportunity for helping others. They seemed to have an answer for every eventuality – every possible dilemma had a policy to cover it so that anxiety and individual response were smothered even before they could be named. However, one or two questions, addressed directly to me, escaped censorship and indicated the possible extent of the students' anxiety about the responsibilities they had undertaken: 'What if you make a mistake?' 'Do you ever think you shouldn't have taken up this work?' 'Can you leave it behind when you go home?'

Groups of counsellors are not immune from the anxiety which gives rise to basic assumption activity. They too may take refuge in dogma or mobilize any of the other ways to avoid thinking which Bion outlined. Here I should like to explore their possible propensity for a way of functioning described by Lawrence *et al.* (1996). In an extremely rich paper these authors take the work of Bion and Turquet further to postulate a fifth basic assumption – of 'me-ness' (baM) – designed to cope with unconscious fears about psychological survival in late modern societies. Basic assumption me-ness is the opposite of Turquet's one-ness. Lawrence *et al.* argue:

> as living in contemporary turbulent societies becomes more risky so the individual is pressed more and more into his or her own inner reality in order to exclude and deny the perceived disturbing realities that are of the outer environment. The inner world becomes thus a comforting one offering succour.
>
> (1996: 33)

They describe the unrest arising from social and political changes in a number of industrialized countries including those of the former Eastern Bloc and conclude:

> the individual loses faith and trust in any structure, whether good or bad, that is greater than the individual. As the environment becomes more persecuting in reality one response is for individuals to make themselves more cut-off from the effects and to withdraw into the inner world of the individual.

They suggest that in the grip of basic assumption me-ness:

> people behave as if the only reality to be considered and taken account of is that of the individual. It is a culture of selfishness in which individuals appear to be only conscious of their own personal boundaries which they believe have to be protected from any incursions by others.
>
> (1996: 36)

They argue that, 'In baM culture the overriding anxiety is that the individual will be lost in the group if it ever emerges' (1996: 36): 'it is as if each individual was a self-contained group acting in its own right' (1996: 37). 'A baM culture is more likely to pay attention to private troubles than ever it would to public issues' (1996: 37). To censure baM functioning is to attack not individuation and personal responsibility but the denial of the possibility of transformation through relatedness with others.

At the time of the consultation I have described, David Armstrong asked if the counselling service was an umbrella under which individuals conducted their private practices or a coherent unit with a shared purpose able to offer a distinct perspective on student experience to the university. His question points to a tension implicit in undertaking work with private issues in a public setting. Counsellors have chosen their profession because they value personal experience, the uniqueness of the individual; their training and own therapy will have reinforced this. Many counsellors are dismissive of organizations, particularly those with a business culture, which they see as imposing stultifying demands on their clients and themselves. Given the difficulties and complexities inherent in working in today's stressed colleges and universities and continued questioning of their credentials, counsellors may be tempted to disengage from their colleagues and institutions and to retreat into the familiarity of their consulting rooms where they may feel more in control and more able to sustain some hope of making a difference. I am suggesting that it would be unfortunate if counsellors' necessary immersion and pleasure in internal worlds and relationships with their clients were to lead them to an overemphasis on individual experience viewed as separate from its social context.

Moreover, disengagement deprives counsellors of information important for understanding their own and their clients' experience. BaM mental states are more likely to flourish in a culture where staff feel too busy to meet for joint reflection and students (because of the growth of part-time attendance, modularized courses, distance learning, competition for jobs, etc.) are less likely to belong to cohesive groups and more likely to be viewed as numbers or consumers. Without remaining open to the pain, confusion and frustration a baM culture can engender (as was attempted in the Armstrong consultation described earlier), counsellors cannot hope to contribute to the development of a more thoughtful, connected approach.

Conclusions: towards integration

The psychological task I am proposing for counsellors is to work with the tensions in their organizations and themselves as well as with those in their clients. I have tried to demonstrate how attention to the prevailing culture in an organization can help in thinking about clinical, training and consultative work and in making links between different experiences. I have suggested that, given current social and cultural trends, counsellors, like their clients, need to work towards integrating or at least tolerating the coexistence of contradictory experiences, holding on to essential values but remaining open to the constant changes and developing possibilities in their organizations and social world. To do this they will need clear but permeable boundaries. They have to hold a difficult balance – offering some stability while retaining curiosity about and openness to the ever-shifting environment in their clients, their institutions and themselves.

Acknowledgements

Writers, like counsellors and clients, do not exist in isolation. The work described here owes much to teachers, supervisors, consultants and colleagues. In particular I should like to thank Dr Judith Trowell and Gail Simmonds for their help with thinking about this chapter.

Bibliography

Armstrong, D. (1991) *The 'Institution in the Mind': Reflections on the Relation of Psycho-Analysis to Work with Institutions*, http://www.human-nature.com/HRAJ/mind.html.

—— (1996) *The Recovery of Meaning*, http://www.human-nature.com/HRAJ/armstron.html.

Bell, E. (1997) 'Counselling in higher education' in S. Palmer (ed.), *Handbook of Counselling*, London: Routledge (1st edn, 1989).

Bion, W. R. (1961) *Experiences in Groups*, London: Tavistock.

Colman, A.D. and Geller, M.H. (eds) (1985) *Group Relations Reader 2*, Washington, DC: A. K. Rice Institute.

Hall, S. (1988) *The Hard Road to Renewal*, London and New York: Verso.

—— (1997) 'Cultural revolutions', *New Statesman*, 5 December.

—— et al. (1992) *Modernity and its Futures*, Cambridge: Polity Press.

Hartley, J. *et al.* (1994) *Key Concepts in Communication and Cultural Studies*, London: Routledge.

Heyno, A. (1997) 'Why do our students fear failure more than they fear death?' *Independent*, 2 October.

Hoggett, P. (1998) 'Hatred of dependency', paper given at the 1998 'Psychoanalysis and the public sphere' conference, University of East London (unpublished).

Kennedy, H. (1997) *Learning Works: Widening Participation in Further Education*, London: FEFC.

Lawrence, W. G., Bain, A. and Gould, L. (1996) 'The fifth basic assumption', *Free Associations*, 6(1): 28–55.

McCaughan, N. and Palmer, B. (1994) *Systems Thinking for Harassed Managers*, London: Karnac.

Moylan, D. (1994) 'The dangers of contagion: projective identification processes in institutions', in A. Obholzer and V. Z. Roberts (eds), *The Unconscious at Work*, London: Routledge.

National Committee of Inquiry into Higher Education: Chairman Sir Ron Dearing (1997) *Higher Education in the Learning Society*, London: HMSO.

Noonan, E. and Spurling, L. (eds) (1992) *The Making of a Counsellor*, London: Routledge.

Obholzer, A. (1994) ' Managing social anxieties in public sector organisations', in A. Obholzer and V. Z. Roberts (eds), *The Unconscious at Work*, London: Routledge.

Smith, E. (ed.) (1997a) *Integrity And Change: Mental Health in the Marketplace*, London: Routledge.

—— (1997b) 'Private selves and shared meanings: forgive us our projections as we forgive those who project into us', *Psychodynamic Counselling*, 3(2): 117–31.

Stokes, J. (1994) 'Institutional chaos and personal stress', in A. Obholzer and V. Z. Roberts (eds), *The Unconscious at Work*, London: Routledge.

Turquet, P. M. (1974) ' Leadership: the individual and the group', in A.D. Colman and M.H. Geller (eds), *Group Relations Reader 2* Washington, DC: A. K. Rice Institute.

White, J. (1997) 'Internal space and the market', in E. Smith (ed.), *Integrity and Change*, London: Routledge.

Williams, R. (1976) *Keywords*, Guildford: Fontana/Croom Helm.

10 Evaluation of clinical counselling in educational settings

Preparing for the future

Lesley Parker

Introduction

Most research hypotheses result from someone asking a question, and the question in turn evolves from curiosity about something observed or thought or felt. Questions that come to mind about evaluating counselling in colleges and universities are:

- Why should we want or need to evaluate counselling in higher and further education?
- What tools do we need to develop to aid evaluation?
- Are counsellors willing to become involved in research and evaluation?

Before attempting to answer these questions, we need to think briefly about the relationship between counselling and research in universities and colleges.

In most institutions, counselling is still a peripheral activity where the practitioners feel under continual pressure to justify what they do, and where the means they use are criticized as not being empirically tested and found valid. Although many of the educational establishments employ and train researchers, the majority of them have not thought about the inappropriateness of traditional approaches, such as randomized control trials, to counselling. Without the development of appropriate tools, managers and researchers will find it difficult to communicate with counsellors about effectiveness, and many counsellors will remain hostile to the idea of research and evaluation.

The case for developing tools has been underlined with the publication of Roth and Fonagy's review of psychotherapy research (1996), with its emphasis on randomized control group trials conducted with selected patients with one identified diagnosis and one treatment method. Such research does not relate to real life in a university or college counselling service: it doesn't address the range of clients, the multiplicity of their concerns, the impact of the institution or the process of learning. Nor does it, generally, allow the clients to have a view on the effectiveness of counselling and their experience of it.

Heppner and colleagues commented on the difficulties of evaluating college counselling in the USA: 'Two major obstacles have been the wide range of problems confronting students, coupled with data that suggest that people engage in different problem-solving for different types of problem' (1994: 315).

What questions do we want evaluation to answer?

Managers will want to know whether counselling is cost-effective – i.e. does it achieve what it sets out to do within the resource limits laid down, and does it do it better than using other forms of pastoral care or than doing nothing? Academic researchers will want to discover a way of measuring the counselling process to show whether outcome is an improvement over the outset. Practitioners will want to be reassured that their clients gain benefit from the process, and may also want to look in depth at what they understand to be happening in terms of their theoretical beliefs. Clients will want reassurance that what they experience in counselling will be beneficial. In looking at this wish-list, we have to take note of the context. Students generally attend university and college in order to learn and/or do research, to fulfil the requirements of a course and gain a qualification. Managers prefer students to be retained in the institution until they successfully complete their academic requirements, if possible in the minimum available time. Counsellors, as well as seeking 'job satisfaction', on the whole wish to see counselling valued as integral to, rather than peripheral to, the educational process.

Some research questions might be:

- What difficulties or concerns do the clients of university and college counselling services have, how serious are they, and does counselling affect them for better or worse?
- What do clients feel about the counselling process? How do they understand it in their academic and institutional context?
- What can practitioners learn from their clients about the clients' perceptions of what counsellors offer in counselling and whether it is helpful?
- What do university and college counsellors claim to do, and do they do it? Do they have any effect on retention rates? Does counselling affect

the academic success of clients? Could anyone else do it as well or more effectively than the counsellor?

Evaluation has been an issue for university and college counsellors since at least the mid-1980s, maybe partly as a result of the emphasis then on total quality management and performance indicators. At that time there were heated discussions over the criteria which HMI inspectors should use for assessing effective counselling and counselling services, and especially over how the assessments should be done. Inspectors asked how they were to assess the counselling process if they didn't sit in on sessions: counsellors stated that to sit in immediately distorted the process, as well as contravening the confidentiality ethic. Ever since that debate there has been a clear need to find a non-intrusive evaluation method that doesn't distort the process. There has been lots of head-scratching and discussion but little concrete progress. Counsellors have become involved in a classic avoidance activity of letting ourselves be diverted into collecting data to evaluate services and the circumstances in which counselling is offered. But what about the counselling itself? Is it satisfactory to rely on supervision, and the monitoring implied in that? Or should we ask counsellors and clients about their experience of the process, and ask them to assess whether it has been worthwhile? Is it necessary to have anyone else's opinion on whether the counselling has been worthwhile? Well, yes! If we are employed by an institution, doing something which involves other members of the institution, then the institution will want to ask questions. What is it that we are doing, with whom, and to what effect?

Efficacy, audit and evaluation

Roth and Fonagy's final conclusion when looking at the implications of their review would not find favour with the majority of counsellors in higher and further education: 'The difficulty in evaluating the efficacy of counselling interventions underscores the need for further standardisation of mental health provision in primary care settings and the rigorous periodic audit of these services by an independent agency' (1996 : 262). Although Roth and Fonagy were referring to counselling in primary health care, such comments might describe the attitude of some educational managers. Many counsellors do not find efficacy studies helpful in guiding everyday practice. As referred to earlier, our clients rarely arrive with only a single issue to work on, most of them would not fit the criteria for inclusion in an efficacy study, and many counsellors would not want to work to the restrictions of a 'scripted' therapeutic intervention. Knowing that a particular therapeutic approach administered over twelve weeks to a bulimic young woman in a research study is more or less effective than treatment with a particular antidepressant does not seem very relevant to working with a young bulimic student who is also cutting herself, and has final exams in four weeks, and is a cause of concern to other students and academic staff.

Similarly, some university counsellors have had painful experience of audit. One service experienced a rigorous audit in 1993 by an independent agency: the counsellors and representatives of the clients felt it to have been irrelevant and potentially damaging in that the audit: (1) failed to understand and take note of the educational context in which counselling took place; (2) didn't take account of the client group's wishes; and (3) made totally unrealistic recommendations about monitoring and outward referral to the NHS. For example, the audit team recommended that students with depression who did not improve after four counselling sessions should be referred to the local NHS out-patient services for CBT – for which at the time there was a waiting list time of over one year!

Maybe evaluation of counselling in educational settings needs to rely more on:

- description of the client and what brought him/her to counselling;
- what would make a beneficial difference to the client;
- how the client and counsellor feel and think about the process;
- the client's 'satisfaction' once counselling has ended.

Description of the client and what brought him/her to counselling

The Association for University and College Counselling (AUCC) has recently developed a categorization system to help in describing what brought the client to counselling, and how severely the client was affected. The lists of categories are derived from a sift of service-developed systems already in use in UK student counselling services in the early 1990s. The system requires counsellors to categorize clients' concerns, both those presented at the initial assessment and those emerging later in the first or subsequent sessions. Counsellors pick a group heading that best describes the concern in its context. They may also select a detailed category if they want further descriptive detail of the issue(s). While doing this, they also think about how serious the concerns are for the client: an assessment of severity is made based on a cluster of factors, and a score or rating given. Severity can be assessed once or several times to show movement in how the client was affected by the concern.

What would make a beneficial difference to the client?

McLeod's definition of outcome is: 'the benefit (or otherwise) and changes observable in clients at the completion of counselling' (1995: 122). So, if one was setting out to do outcome research, clients might be asked before assessment: 'What would make a difference for you that would make you feel counselling has been worthwhile?' The researcher would have to decide whether outcome goals based on such a question should be fixed, or able to vary as counselling proceeds, when often different criteria for 'success' emerge during the work.

Things that clients might feel 'make a difference' could fall into three main groups:

- Aspects of the counselling relationship, such as being taken seriously, being understood, being supported, having time and permission to reflect.
- Understanding the issues, including clarifying things, accepting self, being aware of the impact of the institution and its demands, discovering what caused and what maintains the difficulties.
- Having choices about possible change, possible action, choosing to accept oneself and one's situation – all leading to development of the self that can increase self-esteem and self-confidence.

But how could practitioners research outcome? If we ask clients to define their own 'outcome' goals it will be impossible to look at specific variables across a client population: the best we can achieve is a generalized estimate of satisfaction, and, of course, any satisfaction assessment will be affected by transference in the counselling relationship. The task looks slightly easier if research is done in the context of short-term focused therapy or solution-based therapy where goals are defined. But for other therapies tools that might be used include: standardized self-report inventories (e.g. SCL-90-R which has been used in several university counselling services); client satisfaction questionnaires (there are a variety of individual service-designed examples being used); ratings of target symptoms (e.g. ability to concentrate better); behavioural measures (e.g. grades achieved, number of counselling appointments missed); and structured interviews. All of these attempt to assess a client's conscious aims, and consequent satisfaction or disappointment. What about the unconscious aims underlying embarking on counselling: how can they be described and evaluated?

How the counsellor and client feel and think about the process

It is even more difficult to begin to think about evaluating the process. What do we mean by process? McLeod's way of describing it is that it is made up of a highly complex and elusive set of phenomena which are difficult to observe or measure in an ethical fashion (1995: 143). Some methods have been developed and are described by McLeod (1995: Chapter 9). They include:

- Written accounts by the participants of all or part or certain aspects of the process: this generates a lot of data which is difficult to analyse, and is open to the possibility of significant parts being forgotten or omitted.
- Observation, actual or via audio and/or visual recording: this approach raises questions of ethics, and is felt by many to distort the process it is assessing.
- Interpersonal process recall again involves audio-visual taping: while it can be very informative it is extremely resource-hungry in terms of equipment and time.
- Questionnaires which rate 'standard' parts of the expected process: some in-service designed examples are in use in universities and colleges.
- Client-experience questionnaires which are in essence a debriefing of the actual counselling session.

The client's 'satisfaction' once counselling has ended

There are many examples of evaluation questionnaires in use in university and college counselling services, most of which combine bits of aims, satisfaction, process, etc. An analysis of examples currently in use shows that there are four main types:

- pre-assessment information completed by the client;
- post-assessment information completed by the counsellor;
- post-ending information completed by the counsellor;
- post-ending information completed by the client – this sometimes encompasses elements of pre-counselling information as well.

Lists of the type of information sought appear in Appendix 10.1.

Evaluation questionnaires become useful only if the results are used to improve a counsellor's practice with individual clients, or to consolidate or change what a service or institution offers. For example, looking at problem categories can clarify potential pitfalls for students and staff, and might lead to the development of relevant preventative activities, including leaflet-writing and workshops. Or it could influence how the institution or the service does things or develops services. Similarly, looking at severity might lead to a more realistic view of what counsellors and their clients are having to contend with, with all the consequent implications for resourcing, training and supporting the counsellors. A college recently noted that 40 per cent of its counselled students were categorized as having low mood or depression: this led to a discussion with counsellors of what might underlie this and whether the college could do things to better support such students.

While the above discussion describes what counsellors might think is a good framework for evaluating counselling in colleges and universities, one must ask where it fits in with the manager's need for audit, and desire to know that the counselling is both efficacious and cost-effective. Audit requires a clear statement from a counselling service of its aims and how it intends to meet them, and then a linkage between this and the evaluation method it chooses to show that the counsellors do what they say they do. Managers might also want measures associated with cost-benefit analysis or cost-effectiveness analysis – e.g. comparing retention rates of counselled and non-counselled students, or the grades achieved – or, more contentiously, a reduction in suicidal thought and intention in clients. And they will want to be convinced that an 'in-house' service has cost and other benefits superior to out-placing counselling outside the institution.

The Department of Health, in its document reviewing psychotherapy services in England (1996), is currently trying to adapt 'evidence-based practice' principles to use in evaluating psychological therapies: the hope is that this will provide a rational basis for making clinical decisions about which patient should receive which therapy. The evidence collected to evaluate a particular treatment is based on:

- clinical case description;
- systematic observational studies;
- cohort studies with particular emphasis on outcome;
- non-randomized studies;
- randomized control trials.

How might this be adapted to evaluate counselling interventions with students? An example would be evaluating whether a counselling group for self-selected students requesting help with exam anxiety was effective. The evidence-based evaluation might include:

- descriptions of the students, the degree of anticipatory anxiety they experience, and the effect they believe this has on exam preparation and performance;
- an 'action research' type account of the interventions offered to the group, and how group members reacted and responded;
- measurement of anticipatory anxiety before and after intervention;
- comparison with another group of students with exam anxiety who were only offered a revision workshop;
- assessment of exam performance;
- student evaluation of the effect of the intervention on their anxiety and performance.

Counsellor attitudes to evaluation

The question still needs to be asked: will counsellors in higher and further education be willing to evaluate their counselling? In piloting the AUCC categorization system mentioned above, the development team encountered various reactions from AUCC members asked to define clients' difficulties and the severity of their effect, and we became aware of the influence of counsellors' theoretical perspectives. Some counsellors find it anathemous to categorize at all, alleging that it pathologizes and that that is for psychologists and psychiatrists to do. Some are comfortable describing an event but not 'imposing' their understanding on the student in the form of a label. Others recognize that in assessing a client and his/her situation, there is a sifting process before the description is arrived at, and do not like the reductionism inferred in this. Still others expect that assessment takes into account all that is discovered of a client, and the counselling process, so that the counsellor might make a professionally based judgement of what the issues are – I am quite clear that the latter is the only position a counsellor should hold! In reflecting on the material, in the light of our experience of the relationship and of our past experience, we will make judgements of what we think may be going on: such formulation is not about labelling, or pathologizing, or an abuse of power; it is about making sense of things, and finding a language to describe what we are doing. If we aren't prepared to do that, then of what are we afraid? Of being held accountable for what we do? Of being clear with clients about what is and what is not possible? Of the discipline of approaching our work objectively as well as empathetically?

An account of some of the reactions to the categorization project might give an indication of how counsellors could feel on being asked to evaluate their counselling.

- The development team found the process of categorizing to be very rich. It brought into play all our knowledge and experience: of the field of university and college counselling; of ourselves and our awareness of self; of what the client had told us and what we had observed of the institution, its policy and practice; and of our experience of the counselling relationship. As individual professionals we ended up valuing ourselves and what we offered more.

- Some counsellors were wary of becoming involved in the pilot because they didn't have time. Time to think about our clients! If we don't think we must ask if we are safe to practise at all. We all know of and experience the anxiety and pressure of waiting lists, and the demands of resource-squeezing managements, but counselling is a reflective profession: we must make space to think. We can record the result of that thinking partly in an evaluation system.

- We tried to offer definitions for every heading, and discovered that we couldn't. We could develop a sort of collective, umbrella description if we didn't have to be precise. If we used psychodynamic thinking and language we offended or were incomprehensible to counsellors of other orientations; if we used behavioural thinking and language we were accused of pathologizing. There is not a universally accepted language in which counsellors can describe their work. This implies a grave weakness in attempting any comparative counselling research, because standardized definitions that are meaningful to all cannot be achieved. Thus, any system will be open to varying interpretations of the language used, and like may well not be compared with like – just a somewhat similar like. Does it matter? If you are an empirical scientist familiar with a reductionist use of statistics, as in most of the work reviewed by Roth and Fonagy, yes. If you are an heuristic researcher, no. For most of us it is probably good enough to have things which have at least some elements of similarity grouped together.

- We found that many counsellors were only just beginning to think about how to describe and assess severity. What were we talking about? Seriousness of emotional disturbance? Difficulty of the situation facing the client? The client's emotional robustness? An assessment of functioning? For several years university and college counsellors have talked of clients' difficulties becoming more serious, but haven't defined what they mean. Several of the piloting counsellors were suspicious at first of whether severity rating was possible or useful: the majority reported afterwards that it had been a very helpful thing to do. They had become much clearer about what underlay their impressions of situations being more difficult and clients more disturbed, and this had aided their work with clients. To do the severity rating we adopted the notion of thinking about a cluster of factors, adapted from reading Berman and Jones about risk assessment in mental health practice (1992).

- There was some criticism from some counsellors about any attempt to categorize client issues. To quote from responses to requests for feedback in 1995:

  'the desire for a categorization system marks a step away from person-centredness and non-judgementalism.'
  'Categorization could be inadvertently used to label clients. There is a danger that we will concentrate on treating symptoms, not the underlying causes and distress.'
  'We are not psychiatrists.'
  'Don't use the term "disorder", it's not a counselling word.'
  'We are in danger of falling into the 1990s feeling that things can be put into neat boxes, which somehow denies the necessary anxiety of approaching each client as a unique individual.'

  Could we proceed despite such concerns? We decided that some counsellors would never be ideologically comfortable using any categorization system, and that others 'forget' that not all counsellors share the same theoretical approach or language. We also had some faith that counsellors would not label clients or treat only symptoms. Can we devise evaluation systems that allow for the uniqueness of individuals without jettisoning any attempts at empirical validity in collecting and comparing data?

- The system was found to provide a framework for report writing, especially annual reports. Some services have just reported categories and totals. Others have used correlations and cross-referencing to illustrate particular points that they wish to emphasize. We hope it will allow AUCC to collect national data via its annual survey of services. Given the comments already made about no standard definitions and validity, such data will allow us to say something about how counsellors understand their clients, their clients' situations and the counselling work. We are increasingly asked for such data from government bodies and the press, from researchers, and from services who want to compare their 'picture' with the national picture.

Accessing research

When the research and evaluation is done, we need a way of disseminating it to interested persons. Some journals and publishers may be reluctant to accept such work, just because it may not comply with empirical traditions. But there also seems to be a reluctance of counsellors in higher and further education to publish their work. Many more counsellors are learning research skills and conducting studies as part of higher level courses, and yet it can be very difficult to discover what has been studied and what might be learned from it.

AUCC recently employed a researcher to track down and review research relevant to counselling in post-compulsory education in the UK, and the report was published in mid-1998. The main sources of published research in the UK are: *British Journal of Guidance and Counselling; Journal of Counselling Psychology; Counselling Psychology Quarterly; International Journal for the Advancement of Counselling; Counselling;* and the AUCC newsletter and journal.

But the bulk of research reports are not widely available: they are to be found in the libraries of universities and colleges where researchers studied for higher degrees and postgraduate qualifications. AUCC plans to develop a database of relevant research, based on the 1998 report: how comprehensive it is will depend on authors informing AUCC of their work, and there not being copyright problems in expanding the database.

There are interesting developments occurring in the late 1990s. The Psychological Therapies Research Centre at Leeds University has developed CORE (Clinical Outcomes in Routine Evaluation), a generic counselling evaluation instrument: this is now being piloted in several institutions with additions specific to university and college counselling. CORE is an instrument which addresses global distress and is therefore suitable for use both as an initial screening measure and as an outcome measure. It covers three areas (subjective well-being, symptoms and functioning) and further items to indicate risk/harm. It offers the possibility of national data which will provide the opportunity to develop UK student population norms, and will allow comparative studies to be done.

Universities are procuring external funding to look at several aspects of student experience and difficulty, and the effectiveness or otherwise of counselling and other interventions in enhancing students' functioning.

Thus, the evidence is that university and college counsellors are gradually becoming more involved in research and evaluation. We are beginning to try out and develop acceptable research tools, although there is a lot more to be done in educating those interested in the research results about appropriate methodology for counselling research. We still need to investigate ways to disseminate results. And we still need to persuade and reassure some colleagues that evaluation is part of, not alien to, good ethical professional practice.

At present it is impossible to make a research-based general statement about the clients who use university and college counselling services, about how they experience the counselling and whether it is beneficial: up to now, all we have been able to do is talk about services and their staff. We cannot turn a blind eye to research if we expect resources to continue to be put into counselling services, and if we expect to be able to demonstrate to government and the funding bodies that doing so is a necessary and beneficial expenditure.

APPENDIX 10.1

Information typically sought in evaluation questionnaires devised by university and college counselling services

When questionnaires are composed, they give a range of methods for responses. The question might be open-ended with a blank space for the subject to complete. The subject might be given a range of answers from which to select one or more, by putting a tick in a box. Or the subject might be asked to gauge how much something is relevant by selecting a point on a scale which best describes where they feel they are.

Occasionally, questionnaires to clients ask whether their comments can be quoted anonymously. Most emphasize that the purpose of the questionnaire is to gain information to monitor and if necessary improve the service offered to future clients.

Pre-assessment information completed by the client

Personal information
age
gender
nationality / ethnicity
faculty and course
doctor and any current medication
full- or part-time
under-, post- or non-graduating
disability status

Referral route

Counselling
reasons for coming
expectations

assessment of how severe one's difficulties are
assessment of how well one is coping with the difficulties
effect of the problems on one's life, including academic issues
how long the difficulties have been around
any reservations about counselling

Previous sources of help

Post-assessment information completed by the counsellor

Dates
of referral
of assessment session
of first ongoing session

Previous help in this service
when
how many sessions

Previous help with another agency
when
how many sessions
for how long

Description of
reason for referral
problems with which help is sought
what client has done to cope with or resolve situation
problem categorization and severity rating
risk assessment and action plan

Assessment outcome
no further action
offer ongoing – individual, group, etc.
referral
follow-up
unsuitable for counselling

Post-ending information completed by the counsellor

Time
date ended
total sessions attended, unattended and cancelled
frequency of sessions

Counselling model used
psychodynamic, CBT, etc.

Modality of counselling
individual, group, etc.

Ending
mutually agreed
not mutually agreed
lost touch

Assessment of problem categorization and severity rating

Summary of what are perceived to have been the benefits for the client

Post-ending information completed by the client

Referral
why chose to come to counselling
expectations
problems/well-being: academic, emotional and social
categorization of problems and their severity

Service evaluation
publicity
accessibility and approachability
location
reception
privacy
waiting times and lists
frequency and total number of sessions
helpful non-counselling services – e.g. leaflets, workshops
preferred counsellor – e.g. gender, ethnicity, age

Comments about the counsellor
e.g. understanding, non-judgemental, helpful

*Comments about the counselling process and quality of the counselling
    relationship*

Academic context
links to ability to study
links to academic success
links to remaining in the institution

Ending
reasons for ending
experience of ending

Recommendations
would client recommend service to others?
would client use service again?
has client told people of experience of counselling?
suggestions for improving counselling or the service

Bibliography

BAC (1997) *AUCC Categorisation of Client Issues*, Rugby: BAC.
—— (1998) *Review of Research Relevant to Counselling in UK Colleges and Universities*, Rugby: BAC.
Berman and Jones (1992) 'Adolescent suicide assessment and intervention', *American Psychological Association*.
Bolger, T. (1989) 'Research and evaluation in counselling', in W. Dryden, D. Charles-Edwards and R. Woolfe (eds), *Handbook of Counselling in Britain*, London: Routledge.
Breakwell, G.M. (1987) 'Evaluation of student counselling: a review of the literature 1962–86', *British Journal of Guidance and Counselling*, 15(2): 131–9.
Department of Health (1996) *NHS Psychotherapy Services in England: Review of Strategic Policy*, London: NHS Executive.
Dryden, W. (ed.) (1996) *Research in Counselling and Psychotherapy: Practical Applications*, London: Sage.
Gordon, K. (1992) 'On evaluating UK university counselling services', *ASC Newsletter*, May: 11–24, Rugby: BAC.
Heppner, P., Kivlighan, D., Good, G., Roehlke, H., Hills, H., and Ashby, J. (1994) 'Presenting problems of university counseling center clients: a snapshot and multivariate classification scheme', *Journal of Counseling Psychology*, 41(3): 315–24.
Hooper, R. and Stone, T. (1989) 'A survey of university counselling in the United Kingdom and some observations on evaluation', *British Journal of Guidance and Counselling*, 17(1): 49–58.
Howe, D. (1993) *On Being a Client*, London: Sage.
McLeod, J. (1995) *Doing Counselling Research*, London: Routledge.
Mental Health Foundation (1997) *CORE: Clinical Outcomes in Routine Evaluation*, Leeds: Psychological Therapies Research Centre, University of Leeds.
Robson, C. (1993) *Real World Research*, Oxford: Blackwell.
Roth, A. and Fonagy, P. (1996) *What Works for Whom? A Critical Review of Psychotherapy Research*, New York: Guilford Press.
Sutton, C. (1987) 'The evaluation of counselling: a goal-attainment approach', *Counselling*, 5(1): 35–7.

Index